# CONTENTS

# CONTENTS

## THREE

### FROM Time's Laughingstocks and Other Verses
(PUBLISHED 1909)

# CONTENTS

# FOUR

FROM Satires of Circumstance; Lyrics and Reveries
(PUBLISHED 1914)

# CONTENTS

# CONTENTS

## FIVE

### FROM Moments of Vision and Miscellaneous Verses
### (PUBLISHED 1917)

# CONTENTS

## SIX

### FROM Late Lyrics and Earlier
### (PUBLISHED 1922)

# CONTENTS

## SEVEN

FROM Human Shows, Far Phantasies, Songs, and Trifles
(PUBLISHED 1925)

# CONTENTS

## EIGHT

### FROM Winter Words in Various Moods and Metres
### (PUBLISHED 1928)

# INTRODUCTION

NEARLY a thousand of Thomas Hardy's poems are contained in the Collected Edition, and the number he wrote but did not publish runs to a much larger figure. The bulk of his poetry, and the best of it, moreover, was written in his sixties, seventies, and even eighties, and as late as 1927, at the age of eighty-six, he was still writing poems for his last volume, *Winter Words*, which appeared posthumously. His reputation as a novelist had been established, not without controversy and harsh criticism, by the time he turned, once and for all, to poetry, after the publication of his great novels, *The Mayor of Casterbridge*, *The Return of the Native*, *Tess of the d'Urbervilles*, and *Jude the Obscure*. There have been relatively few poet-novelists in English literature. Most of them – such as Scott, Emily Brontë, Meredith, Kipling, Belloc, and Chesterton – have excelled either as poets or as novelists but seldom as both. The only authentic double-firsts in this field are, I believe, Hardy and D. H. Lawrence.

By all accounts Hardy was a sympathetic and attractive personality. There are many witnesses to his kindliness and his delicacy of feeling, his devotion to the people and the traditions of his native Dorsetshire. His entire work, and his own comments upon it, show, too, that he was a dedicated man of letters, following no literary fashions and seeking no literary ambitions in the fulfilment of his mission as a writer. One of the favourite occupations of a certain kind of scholar is to detect the 'influences' revealed by a writer's work, to ferret out the clues which show how and where he assimilated other styles into his own. As C. Day Lewis has so aptly said: 'Influence-spotters don't have a very happy time with him.' Hardy's poems, like his novels, derive from his own nature, experience, and integrity, and it is this characteristic which makes his testimony so personal and so moving.

The shorthand in which Hardy has so often been summed up in his life, and since, was 'pessimist'. A tender and com-

passionate nature can scarcely avoid having a sombre outlook on life and there is a world of difference between the melancholy and the morbid, although those who knew him best were aware of a morbid streak in Hardy. Yet although he found no particular relish in relating the misfortunes or frustrations of human life, he was constantly conscious that nature is indifferent to our aspirations and sufferings. Despite his affection for the Church and its associations, the conventional consolations of religion had no meaning for him, yet his adherence to agnosticism was as profound and sincere an expression of faith as any felt and practised by an orthodox conformist to any positive religion. It speaks well for England that the ashes of this uncompromising determinist should have been laid at last in Westminster Abbey.

Hardy was sensitive to this reiterated charge of pessimism, and insisted that he was doing no more than put out 'questionings in the exploration of reality':

*If way to the Better there be, it exacts a full look at the Worst.* He disclaimed any made-up attitude to life. In the short preface which he had written, shortly before his death, for *Winter Words*, he declared: 'no harmonious philosophy is attempted in these pages – or in any bygone pages of mine, for that matter.' He did not seek to project a doctrine but to discover varieties of evidence about human behaviour and destiny. In an earlier preface (to *Poems of the Past and the Present*) he had written, 'Unadjusted impressions have their value, and the road to a true philosophy of life seems to lie in humbly recording diverse readings of its phenomena as they are forced upon us by chance and change.'

For these disclaimers of any intention of projecting a philosophy, as Wordsworth or Tennyson had done, Hardy's word must be accepted. Nevertheless, his persistent method of recording in his poems 'unadjusted impressions' of life and experience accumulated a body of poetry which is on the whole melancholy although not infrequently relieved by moods of ecstasy and humour. Whether he reached his sombre conclusions by accident or by design cannot much matter to those who read him, any more than it matters

# I

*from*

## WESSEX POEMS AND
## OTHER VERSES

THE PENGUIN POETS

D53

THOMAS HARDY

Very few great novelists have also been great poets. One English writer who achieved this rare double distinction was Thomas Hardy (1840–1928) who, after making his name with such famous novels as *The Mayor of Casterbridge*, *The Return of the Native*, and *Jude the Obscure*, turned to poetry and wrote nothing but poetry for the rest of his long life.

Hardy disclaimed any intention of using poetry to express some particular point of view. His purpose, he said, was to record in the rhythm and music of verse impressions of what he saw and remembered about nature and human nature, and in that sense his poetry is the diary of an observant and compassionate countryman. Hardy spent most of his life in Dorset, and those who know and enjoy the characteristic landscape and people of Hardy's Wessex novels will find similar scenes and personalities in his poems.

This selection has been chosen from the *Collected Poems* (Macmillan) by Sir William Emrys Williams, a Director of Penguin Books and Secretary-General of the Arts Council of Great Britain. Other poets he has edited for Penguins include D. H. Lawrence, Robert Browning, Tennyson, and Wordsworth.

FOR
J.M.L.

Penguin Books Ltd, Harmondsworth, Middlesex
AUSTRALIA: Penguin Books Pty Ltd, 762 Whitehorse Road,
Mitcham, Victoria

—

*Collected Poems* first published 1919
Second, third, and fourth editions incorporating later works
1923, 1928, and 1930 respectively
This selection first published 1960

—

Made and printed in Great Britain
by Unwin Brothers Ltd
Woking and London

# Thomas Hardy

*A Selection of Poems Chosen and Edited by*

## W. E. WILLIAMS

PENGUIN BOOKS

# A CONFESSION TO A FRIEND IN
## TROUBLE

Your troubles shrink not, though I feel them less
Here, far away, than when I tarried near;
I even smile old smiles – with listlessness –
Yet smiles they are, not ghastly mockeries mere.

A thought too strange to house within my brain
Haunting its outer precincts I discern:
– *That I will not show zeal again to learn*
*Your griefs, and, sharing them, renew my pain* . . .

It goes, like murky bird or buccaneer
That shapes its lawless figure on the main,
And staunchness tends to banish utterly
The unseemly instinct that had lodgement here;
Yet, comrade old, can bitterer knowledge be
Than that, though banned, such instinct was in me!

*1866*


## SHE AT HIS FUNERAL

They bear him to his resting-place –
In slow procession sweeping by;
I follow at a stranger's space;
His kindred they, his sweetheart I.
Unchanged my gown of garish dye,
Though sable-sad is their attire;
But they stand round with griefless eye,
Whilst my regret consumes like fire!

*187–*

## SHE, TO HIM

### I

When you shall see me in the toils of Time,
My lauded beauties carried off from me,
My eyes no longer stars as in their prime,
My name forgot of Maiden Fair and Free;

When, in your being, heart concedes to mind,
And judgement, though you scarce its process know,
Recalls the excellencies I once enshrined,
And you are irked that they have withered so:

Remembering mine the loss is, not the blame,
That Sportsman Time but rears his brood to kill,
Knowing me in my soul the very same –
One who would die to spare you touch of ill! –
Will you not grant to old affection's claim
The hand of friendship down Life's sunless hill?

*1866*

## SHE, TO HIM

### II

Perhaps, long hence, when I have passed away,
Some other's feature, accent, thought like mine,
Will carry you back to what I used to say,
And bring some memory of your love's decline.

Then you may pause awhile and think, 'Poor jade!'
And yield a sigh to me – as ample due,
Not as the tittle of a debt unpaid
To one who could resign her all to you –

And thus reflecting, you will never see
That your thin thought, in two small words conveyed,
Was no such fleeting phantom-thought to me,
But the Whole Life wherein my part was played;
And you amid its fitful masquerade
A Thought – as I in your life seem to be!

*1866*

## SHE, TO HIM

### III

I will be faithful to thee; aye, I will!
And Death shall choose me with a wondering eye
That he did not discern and domicile
One his by right ever since that last Good-bye!

I have no care for friends, or kin, or prime
Of manhood who deal gently with me here;
Amid the happy people of my time
Who work their love's fulfilment, I appear

Numb as a vane that cankers on its point,
True to the wind that kissed ere canker came:
Despised by souls of Now, who would disjoint
The mind from memory, making Life all aim,

My old dexterities in witchery gone,
And nothing left for Love to look upon.

*1866*

## SHE, TO HIM

### IV

This love puts all humanity from me;
I can but maledict her, pray her dead,
For giving love and getting love of thee –
Feeding a heart that else mine own had fed!

How much I love I know not, life not known,
Save as one unit I would add love by;
But this I know, my being is but thine own –
Fused from its separateness by ecstasy.

And thus I grasp thy amplitudes, of her
Ungrasped, though helped by nigh-regarding eyes;
Canst thou then hate me as an envier
Who see unrecked what I so dearly prize?
Believe me, Lost One, Love is lovelier
The more it shapes its moan in selfish-wise.

*1866*

# FRIENDS BEYOND

William Dewy, Tranter Reuben, Farmer Ledlow late at
    plough,
    Robert's kin, and John's, and Ned's,
And the Squire, and Lady Susan, lie in Mellstock churchyard
    now!

'Gone', I call them, gone for good, that group of local hearts
    and heads;
    Yet at mothy curfew-tide,
And at midnight when the noon-heat breathes it back from
    walls and leads,

They've a way of whispering to me – fellow-wight who yet
    abide –
    In the muted, measured note
Of a ripple under archways, or a lone cave's stillicide:

'We have triumphed: this achievement turns the bane to
    antidote,
    Unsuccesses to success,
Many thought-worn eyes and morrows to a morrow free of
    thought.

'No more need we corn and clothing, feel of old terrestial
    stress;
    Chill detraction stirs no sigh;
Fear of death has even bygone us: death gave all that we
    possess.'

W.D.: 'Ye mid burn the old bass-viol that I set such value by.'
SQUIRE: 'You may hold the manse in fee,
    You may wed my spouse, may let my children's
    memory of me die.'

LADY S.: 'You may have my rich brocades, my laces; take each
    household key;
        Ransack coffer, desk, bureau;
    Quiz the few poor treasures hid there, con the letters
    kept by me.'

FAR.: 'Ye mid zell my favourite heifer, ye mid let the charlock
    grow,
        Foul the grinterns, give up thrift.'

FAR. WIFE: 'If ye break my best blue china, children, I shan't
    care or ho.'

ALL: 'We've no wish to hear the tidings, how the people's
    fortunes shift;
        What your daily doings are;
    Who are wedded, born, divided; if your lives beat slow
    or swift.

'Curious not the least are we if our intents you make or mar,
    If you quire to our old tune,
If the City stage still passes, if the weirs still roar afar.'

– Thus, with very gods' composure, freed those crosses late
    and soon
        Which, in life, the Trine allow
(Why, none witteth), and ignoring all that haps beneath the
    moon,

William Dewy, Tranter Reuben, Farmer Ledlow late at
    plough,
        Robert's kin, and John's, and Ned's,
And the Squire, and Lady Susan, murmur mildly to me now.

# THOMAS HARDY

# THE IMPERCIPIENT

## (AT A CATHEDRAL SERVICE)

That with this bright believing band
    I have no claim to be,
That faiths by which my comrades stand
    Seem fantasies to me,
And mirage-mists their Shining Land,
    Is a strange destiny.

Why thus my soul should be consigned
    To infelicity,
Why always I must feel as blind
    To sights my brethren see,
Why joys they've found I cannot find,
    Abides a mystery.

Since heart of mine knows not that ease
    Which they know; since it be
That He who breathes All's Well to these
    Breathes no All's-Well to me,
My lack might move their sympathies
    And Christian charity!

I am like a gazer who should mark
    An inland company
Standing upfingered, with, 'Hark! hark!
    The glorious distant sea!'
And feel, 'Alas, 'tis but yon dark
    And wind-swept pine to me!'

Yet I would bear my shortcomings
    With meet tranquillity,
But for the charge that blessed things
    I'd liefer not have be.

O, doth a bird deprived of wings
    Go earth-bound wilfully!

    .     .     .     .

Enough. As yet disquiet clings
About us. Rest shall we.

# THE BRIDE-NIGHT FIRE

## (A WESSEX TRADITION)

They had long met o' Zundays – her true love and she –
  And at junketings, maypoles, and flings;
But she bode wi' a thirtover[1] uncle, and he
Swore by noon and by night that her goodman should be
Naibour Sweatley – a wight often weak at the knee
From taking o' sommat more cheerful than tea –
  Who tranted,[2] and moved people's things.

She cried, 'O pray pity me!' Nought would he hear;
  Then with wild rainy eyes she obeyed.
She chid when her Love was for clinking off wi' her:
The pa'son was told, as the season drew near,
To throw over pu'pit the names of the pair
  As fitting one flesh to be made.

The wedding-day dawned and the morning drew on;
  The couple stood bridegroom and bride;
The evening was passed, and when midnight had gone
The feasters horned,[3] 'God save the King', and anon
  The pair took their homealong[4] ride.

The lover Tim Tankens mourned heart-sick and leer[5]
  To be thus of his darling deprived:
He roamed in the dark ath'art field, mound, and mere,
And, a'most without knowing it, found himself near
The house of the tranter, and now of his Dear,
  Where the lantern-light showed 'em arrived.

---

1 *thirtover*, cross.      3 *horned*, sang loudly.
2 *tranted*, traded as carrier.    4 *homealong*, homeward.
        5 *leer*, empty-stomached.

The bride sought her chamber so calm and so pale
   That a Northern had thought her resigned;
But to eyes that had seen her in tidetimes[1] of weal,
Like the white cloud o' smoke, the red battlefield's vail,
   That look spak' of havoc behind.

The bridegroom yet laitered a beaker to drain,
   Then reeled to the linhay[2] for more,
When the candle-snoff kindled some chaff from his grain –
Flames spread, and red vlankers[3] wi' might and wi' main
   Around beams, thatch, and chimley-tun[4] roar.

Young Tim away yond, rafted[5] up by the light,
   Through brimbles and underwood tears,
Till he comes to the orchet, when crooping[6] from sight
In the lewth[7] of a codlin-tree, bivering[8] wi' fright,
Wi' on'y her night-rail to cover her plight,
   His lonesome young Barbree appears.

Her cwold little figure half-naked he views
   Played about by the frolicsome breeze,
Her light-tripping totties,[9] her ten little tooes,
All bare and besprinkled wi' Fall's[10] chilly dews,
While her great gallied[11] eyes through her hair hanging loose
   Shone as stars through a tardle[12] o' trees.

She eyed him; and, as when a weir-hatch is drawn,
   Her tears, penned by terror afore,
With a rushing of sobs in a shower were strawn,
Till her power to pour 'em seemed wasted and gone
   From the heft[13] o' misfortune she bore.

---

| | |
|---|---|
| 1 *tidetimes*, holidays. | 7 *lewth*, shelter. |
| 2 *linhay*, lean-to building. | 8 *bivering*, with chattering teeth. |
| 3 *vlankers*, fire-flakes. | 9 *totties*, feet. |
| 4 *chimley-tun*, chimney-stack. | 10 *Fall*, autumn. |
| 5 *rafted*, roused. | 11 *gallied*, frightened. |
| 6 *crooping*, squatting down. | 12 *tardle*, entanglement. |

13 *heft*, weight.

ʹO Tim, my *own* Tim I must call ʼee – I will!
  All the world has turned round on me so!
Can you help her who loved ʼee, though acting so ill?
Can you pity her misery – feel for her still?
When worse than her body so quivering and chill
  Is her heart in its winter oʼ woe!

ʻI think I mid¹ almost haʼ borne it,ʼ she said,
  ʻHad my griefs one by one come to hand;
But O, to be slave to thik husbird,² for bread,
And then, upon top oʼ that, driven to wed,
And then, upon top oʼ that, burnt out oʼ bed,
  Is more than my nater can stand!ʼ

Like a lion ʼithin en Timʼs spirit outsprung –
(Tim had a great soul when his feelings were wrung) –
  ʻFeel for ʼee, dear Barbree?ʼ he cried;
And his warm working-jacket then straightway he flung
Round about her, and horsed her by jerks, till she clung
Like a chiel on a gipsy, her figure uphung
  By the sleeves that he tightly had tied.

Over piggeries, and mixens,³ and apples, and hay,
  They lumpered⁴ straight into the night;
And finding ere long where a halter-path⁵ lay,
Sighted Timʼs house by dawn, onʼy seen on their way
By a naibour or two who were up wiʼ the day,
  But who gathered no clue to the sight.

Then tender Tim Tankens he searched here and there
  For some garment to clothe her fair skin;
But though he had breeches and waistcoats to spare,
He had nothing quite seemly for Barbree to wear,
Who, half shrammed⁶ to death, stood and cried on a chair
  At the caddle⁷ she found herself in.

---

| | |
|---|---|
| 1 *mid*, might. | 4 *lumpered*, stumbled. |
| 2 *thik husbird*, that rascal. | 5 *halter-path*, bridle-path. |
| 3 *mixens*, manure-heaps. | 6 *shrammed*, numbed. |

7 *caddle*, quandary.

31

There was one thing to do, and that one thing he did,
   He lent her some clothes of his own,
And she took 'em perforce; and while swiftly she slid
Them upon her Tim turned to the winder, as bid,
Thinking, 'O that the picter my duty keeps hid
   To the sight o' my eyes mid[1] be shown!'

In the tallet[2] he stowed her; there huddied[3] she lay,
   Shortening sleeves, legs, and tails to her limbs;
But most o' the time in a mortal bad way,
Well knowing that there'd be the divel to pay
If 'twere found that, instead o' the element's prey,
   She was living in lodgings at Tim's.

'Where's the tranter?' said men and boys; 'where can he be?'
   'Where's the tranter?' said Barbree alone.
'Where on e'th is the tranter?' said everybod-y:
They sifted the dust of his perished roof-tree,
   And all they could find was a bone.

Then the uncle cried, 'Lord, pray have mercy on me!'
   And in terror began to repent.
But before 'twas complete, and till sure she was free,
Barbree drew up her loft-ladder, tight turned her key –
Tim bringing up breakfast and dinner and tea –
   Till the news of her hiding got vent.

Then followed the custom-kept rout, shout, and flare
Of a skimmity-ride[4] through the naibourhood, ere
   Folk had proof o' wold[5] Sweatley's decay.
Whereupon decent people all stood in a stare,
Saying Tim and his lodger should risk it, and pair:
So he took her to church. An' some laughing lads there
Cried to Tim, 'After Sweatley!' She said, 'I declare
   I stand as a maiden today!'

    *Written 1866, printed 1875*

| | |
|---|---|
| 1 *mid*, might. | 4 *skimmity-ride*, satirical procession |
| 2 *tallet*, loft. |    with effigies. |
| 3 *huddied*, hidden. | 5 *wold*, old. |

## 'I LOOK INTO MY GLASS'

I look into my glass,
And view my wasting skin,
And say, 'Would God it came to pass
My heart had shrunk as thin!'

For then, I, undistrest
By hearts grown cold to me,
Could lonely wait my endless rest
With equanimity.

But Time, to make me grieve,
Part steals, lets part abide;
And shakes this fragile frame at eve
With throbbings of noontide.

# 2

*from*

POEMS OF THE PAST AND THE
PRESENT

# A CHRISTMAS GHOST-STORY

South of the Line, inland from far Durban,
A mouldering soldier lies – your countryman.
Awry and doubled up are his gray bones,
And on the breeze his puzzled phantom moans
Nightly to clear Canopus: 'I would know
By whom and when the All-Earth-gladdening Law
Of Peace, brought in by that Man Crucified,
Was ruled to be inept, and set aside?
And what of logic or of truth appears
In tacking "Anno Domini" to the years?
Near twenty-hundred liveried thus have hied,
But tarries yet the Cause for which He died.'

*Christmas Eve 1899*

# DRUMMER HODGE

### I

They throw in Drummer Hodge, to rest
    Uncoffined – just as found:
His landmark is a kopje-crest
    That breaks the veldt around;
And foreign constellations west
    Each night above his mound.

### II

Young Hodge the Drummer never knew –
    Fresh from his Wessex home –
The meaning of the broad Karoo,
    The Bush, the dusty loam,
And why uprose to nightly view
    Strange stars amid the gloam.

### III

Yet portion of that unknown plain
        Will Hodge for ever be;
His homely Northern breast and brain
        Grow to some Southern tree,
And strange-eyed constellations reign
        His stars eternally.


# THE SOULS OF THE SLAIN

### I

The thick lids of Night closed upon me
        Alone at the Bill
        Of the Isle by the Race[1] –
Many-caverned, bald, wrinkled of face –
And with darkness and silence the spirit was on me
        To brood and be still.


### II

No wind fanned the flats of the ocean,
        Or promontory sides,
        Or the ooze by the strand,
    Or the bent-bearded slope of the land,
Whose base took its rest amid everlong motion
        Of criss-crossing tides.


### III

Soon from out of the Southward seemed nearing
        A whirr, as of wings
        Waved by mighty-vanned flies,
    Or by night-moths of measureless size,
And in softness and smoothness well-nigh beyond hearing
        Of corporal things.

1 The 'Race' is a turbulent sea-area off the Bill of Portland, where
contrary tides meet.

IV

And they bore to the bluff, and alighted –
    A dim-discerned train
    Of sprites without mould,
Frameless souls none might touch or might hold –
On the ledge by the turreted lantern, far-sighted
    By men of the main.


V

And I heard them say 'Home!' and I knew them
    For souls of the felled
    On the earth's nether bord
Under Capricorn, whither they'd warred,
And I neared in my awe, and gave heedfulness to them
    With breathings inheld.


VI

Then, it seemed, there approached from the northward
    A senior soul-flame
    Of the like filmy hue:
And he met them and spake: 'Is it you,
O my men?' Said they, 'Aye! We bear homeward and hearth-
    ward
    To feast on our fame!'


VII

'I've flown there before you,' he said then:
    'Your households are well;
    But – your kin linger less
On your glory and war-mightiness
Than on dearer things.' – 'Dearer?' cried these from the dead
    then,
    'Of what do they tell?'

### VIII

'Some mothers muse sadly, and murmur
    Your doings as boys –
    Recall the quaint ways
Of your babyhood's innocent days.
Some pray that, ere dying, your faith had grown firmer,
    And higher your joys.

### IX

'A father broods: "Would I had set him
    To some humble trade,
    And so slacked his high fire,
And his passionate martial desire;
And told him no stories to woo him and whet him
    To this dire crusade!"'

### X

'And, General, how hold out our sweethearts,
    Sworn loyal as doves?'
    – 'Many mourn; many think
It is not unattractive to prink
Them in sables for heroes. Some fickle and fleet hearts
    Have found them new loves.'

### XI

'And our wives?' quoth another resignedly,
    'Dwell they on our deeds?'
    – 'Deeds of home; that live yet
Fresh as new – deeds of fondness or fret;
Ancient words that were kindly expressed or unkindly,
    These, these have their heeds.'

### XII

– 'Alas! then it seems that our glory
    Weighs less in their thought
    Than our old homely acts,
And the long-ago commonplace facts
Of our lives – held by us as scarce part of our story,
    And rated as nought!'

XIII

Then bitterly some: 'Was it wise now
      To raise the tomb-door
      For such knowledge? Away!'
   But the rest: 'Fame we prized till today;
Yet that hearts keep us green for old kindness we prize now
      A thousand times more!'

XIV

Thus speaking, the trooped apparitions
      Began to disband
      And resolve them in two:
   Those whose record was lovely and true
Bore to northward for home: those of bitter traditions
      Again left the land,

XV

And, towering to seaward in legions,
      They paused at a spot
      Overbending the Race
   That engulphing, ghast, sinister place –
Whither headlong they plunged, to the fathomless regions
      Of myriads forgot.

XVI

And the spirits of those who were homing
      Passed on, rushingly,
      Like the Pentecost Wind;
   And the whirr of their wayfaring thinned
And surceased on the sky, and but left in the gloaming
      Sea-mutterings and me.

*December 1899*

# SHELLEY'S SKYLARK

*(The neighbourhood of Leghorn: March 1887)*

Somewhere afield here something lies
In Earth's oblivious eyeless trust
That moved a poet to prophecies –
A pinch of unseen, unguarded dust:

The dust of the lark that Shelley heard,
And made immortal through times to be; –
Though it only lived like another bird,
And knew not its immortality:

Lived its meek life; then, one day, fell –
A little ball of feather and bone;
And how it perished, when piped farewell,
And where it wastes, are alike unknown.

Maybe it rests in the loam I view,
Maybe it throbs in a myrtle's green,
Maybe it sleeps in the coming hue
Of a grape on the slopes of yon inland scene.

Go find it, faeries, go and find
That tiny pinch of priceless dust,
And bring a casket silver-lined,
And framed of gold that gems encrust;

And we will lay it safe therein,
And consecrate it to endless time;
For it inspired a bard to win
Ecstatic heights in thought and rhyme.

## TO LIFE

O Life with the sad seared face,
    I weary of seeing thee,
And thy draggled cloak, and thy hobbling pace,
    And thy too-forced pleasantry!

I know what thou would'st tell
    Of Death, Time, Destiny –
I have known it long, and know, too, well
    What it all means for me.

But canst thou not array
    Thyself in rare disguise,
And feign like truth, for one mad day,
    That Earth is Paradise?

I'll tune me to the mood,
    And mumm with thee till eve;
And maybe what as interlude
    I feign, I shall believe!

## THE SLEEP-WORKER

When wilt thou wake, O Mother, wake and see –
As one who, held in trance, has laboured long
By vacant rote and prepossession strong –
The coils that thou hast wrought unwittingly;

Wherein have place, unrealized by thee,
Fair growths, foul cankers, right enmeshed with wrong,
Strange orchestras of victim-shriek and song,
And curious blends of ache and ecstasy? –

Should that morn come, and show thy opened eyes
All that Life's palpitating tissues feel,
How wilt thou bear thyself in thy surprise? –

43

Wilt thou destroy, in one wild shock of shame,
Thy whole high heaving firmamental frame,
Or patiently adjust, amend, and heal?

# TO AN UNBORN PAUPER CHILD

### I

Breathe not, hid Heart: cease silently,
And though thy birth-hour beckons thee,
    Sleep the long sleep:
    The Doomsters heap
Travails and teens around us here,
And Time-wraiths turn our songsingings to fear.

### II

Hark, how the peoples surge and sigh,
And laughters fail, and greetings die:
    Hopes dwindle; yea,
    Faiths waste away,
Affections and enthusiasms numb;
Thou canst not mend these things if thou dost come.

### III

Had I the ear of wombèd souls
Ere their terrestrial chart unrolls,
    And thou wert free
    To cease, or be,
Then would I tell thee all I know,
And put it to thee: Wilt thou take Life so?

### IV

Vain vow! No hint of mine may hence
To theeward fly: to thy locked sense
    Explain none can
    Life's pending plan:
Thou wilt thy ignorant entry make
Though skies spout fire and blood and nations quake.

V

Fain would I, dear, find some shut plot
Of earth's wide wold for thee, where not
  One tear, one qualm,
  Should break the calm.
But I am weak as thou and bare;
No man can change the common lot to rare.

VI

Must come and bide. And such are we –
Unreasoning, sanguine, visionary –
  That I can hope
  Health, love, friends, scope
In full for thee; can dream thou'lt find
Joys seldom yet attained by humankind!

## TO LIZBIE BROWNE

I

Dear Lizbie Browne,
Where are you now?
In sun, in rain? –
Or is your brow
Past joy, past pain,
Dear Lizbie Browne?

II

Sweet Lizbie Browne,
How you could smile,
How you could sing!
How archly wile
In glance-giving,
Sweet Lizbie Browne!

45

### III

And, Lizbie Browne,
Who else had hair
Bay-red as yours,
Or flesh so fair
Bred out of doors,
Sweet Lizbie Browne?

### IV

When, Lizbie Browne,
You had just begun
To be endeared
By stealth to one,
You disappeared
My Lizbie Browne!

### V

Ay, Lizbie Browne,
So swift your life,
And mine so slow,
You were a wife
Ere I could show
Love, Lizbie Browne.

### VI

Still, Lizbie Browne,
You won, they said,
The best of men
When you were wed. . . .
Where went you then,
O Lizbie Browne?

### VII

Dear Lizbie Browne,
I should have thought,
'Girls ripen fast',

And coaxed and caught
You ere you passed,
Dear Lizbie Browne!

### VIII

But, Lizbie Browne,
I let you slip;
Shaped not a sign;
Touched never your lip
With lip of mine,
Lost Lizbie Browne!

### IX

So, Lizbie Browne,
When on a day
Men speak of me
As not, you'll say,
'And who was he?' –
Yes, Lizbie Browne!

## THE WELL-BELOVED

I went by star and planet shine
    Towards the dear one's home
At Kingsbere, there to make her mine
    When the next sun upclomb.

I edged the ancient hill and wood
    Beside the Ikling Way,
Nigh where the Pagan temple stood
    In the world's earlier day.

And as I quick and quicker walked
    On gravel and on green,
I sang to sky, and tree, or talked
    Of her I called my queen.

47

– 'O faultless is her dainty form,
    And luminous her mind;
She is the God-created norm
    Of perfect womankind!'

A shape whereon one star-blink gleamed
    Slid softly by my side,
A woman's; and her motion seemed
    The motion of my bride.

And yet methought she'd drawn erstwhile
    Out from the ancient leaze,
Where once were pile and peristyle
    For men's idolatries.

– 'O maiden lithe and lone, what may
    Thy name and lineage be
Who so resemblest by this ray
    My darling? – Art thou she?'

The Shape: 'Thy bride remains within
    Her father's grange and grove.'
– 'Thou speakest rightly,' I broke in,
    'Thou art not she I love.'

– 'Nay: though thy bride remains inside
    Her father's walls', said she,
'The one most dear is with thee here,
    For thou dost love but me.'

Then I: 'But she, my only choice,
    Is now at Kingsbere Grove?'
Again her soft mysterious voice:
    'I am thy only Love.'

Thus still she vouched, and still I said,
    'O sprite, that cannot be!' . . .
It was as if my bosom bled,
    So much she troubled me.

The sprite resumed: 'Thou hast transferred
    To her dull form awhile
My beauty, fame, and deed, and word,
    My gestures and my smile.

'O fatuous man, this truth infer,
    Brides are not what they seem;
Thou lovest what thou dreamest her;
    I am thy very dream!'

– 'O then', I answered miserably,
    Speaking as scarce I knew,
'My loved one, I must wed with thee
    If what thou sayest be true!'

She, proudly, thinning in the gloom:
    'Though, since troth-plight began,
I have ever stood as bride to groom,
    I wed no mortal man!'

Thereat she vanished by the lane
    Adjoining Kingsbere town,
Near where, men say, once stood the Fane
    To Venus, on the Down.

– When I arrived and met my bride
    Her look was pinched and thin,
As if her soul had shrunk and died,
    And left a waste within.

# A BROKEN APPOINTMENT

You did not come,
And marching Time drew on, and wore me numb. –
Yet less for loss of your dear presence there
Than that I thus found lacking in your make
That high compassion which can overbear
Reluctance for pure lovingkindness' sake
Grieved I, when, as the hope-hour stroked its sum,
You did not come.

You love not me,
And love alone can lend you loyalty;
– I know and knew it. But, unto the store
Of human deeds divine in all but name,
Was it not worth a little hour or more
To add yet this: Once you, a woman, came
To soothe a time-torn man; even though it be
You love not me?

# THE SUPERSEDED

## I

As newer comers crowd the fore,
    We drop behind.
– We who have laboured long and sore
    Times out of mind,
And keen are yet, must not regret
    To drop behind.

## II

Yet there are some of us who grieve
    To go behind;
Staunch, strenuous souls who scarce believe
    Their fires declined,
And know none spares, remembers, cares
    Who go behind.

III

'Tis not that we have unforetold
    The drop behind;
We feel the new must oust the old
    In every kind;
But yet we think, must we, must *we*,
    Too, drop behind?

## THE DARKLING THRUSH

I leant upon a coppice gate
    When Frost was spectre-gray,
And Winter's dregs made desolate
    The weakening eye of day.
The tangled bine-stems scored the sky
    Like strings of broken lyres,
And all mankind that haunted nigh
    Had sought their household fires.

The land's sharp features seemed to be
    The Century's corpse outleant,
His crypt the cloudy canopy,
    The wind his death-lament.
The ancient pulse of germ and birth
    Was shrunken hard and dry,
And every spirit upon earth
    Seemed fervourless as I.

At once a voice arose among
    The bleak twigs overhead
In a full-hearted evensong
    Of joy illimited;
An aged thrush, frail, gaunt, and small,
    In blast-beruffled plume,
Had chosen thus to fling his soul
    Upon the growing gloom.

So little cause for carolings
    Of such ecstatic sound
Was written on terrestrial things
    Afar or nigh around,
That I could think there trembled through
    His happy good-night air
Some blessed Hope, whereof he knew
    And I was unaware.

*31 December 1900*

# THE MILKMAID

    Under a daisied bank
There stands a rich red ruminating cow,
    And hard against her flank
A cotton-hooded milkmaid bends her brow.

    The flowery river-ooze
Upheaves and falls; the milk purrs in the pail;
    Few pilgrims but would choose
The peace of such a life in such a vale.

    The maid breathes words – to vent,
It seems, her sense of Nature's scenery,
    Of whose life, sentiment,
And essence, very part itself is she.

    She bends a glance of pain,
And, at a moment, lets escape a tear;
    Is it that passing train,
Whose alien whirr offends her country ear? –

    Nay! Phyllis does not dwell
On visual and familiar things like these;
    What moves her is the spell
Of inner themes and inner poetries:

Could but by Sunday morn
Her gay new gown come, meads might dry to dun.
Trains shriek till ears were torn,
If Fred would not prefer that Other One.


# THE RUINED MAID

'O 'Melia, my dear, this does everything crown!
Who could have supposed I should meet you in Town?
And whence such fair garments, such prosperi-ty?' –
'O didn't you know I'd been ruined?' said she.

– 'You left us in tatters, without shoes or socks,
Tired of digging potatoes, and spudding up docks;
And now you've gay bracelets and bright feathers three!' –
'Yes: that's how we dress when we're ruined', said she.

– 'At home in the barton you said "thee" and "thou",
And "thik oon", and "theäs oon", and "t'other"; but now
Your talking quite fits 'ee for high compa-ny!' –
'Some polish is gained with one's ruin', said she.

– 'Your hands were like paws then, your face blue and bleak
But now I'm bewitched by your delicate cheek,
And your little gloves fit as on any la-dy!' –
'We never do work when we're ruined', said she.

– 'You used to call home-life a hag-ridden dream,
And you'd sigh, and you'd sock; but at present you seem
To know not of megrims or melancho-ly!' –
'True. One's pretty lively when ruined', said she.

– 'I wish I had feathers, a fine sweeping gown,
And a delicate face, and could strut about Town!' –
'My dear – a raw country girl, such as you be,
Cannot quite expect that. You ain't ruined', said she.

*Westbourne Park Villas, 1866*

# ] THE SELF-UNSEEING

Here is the ancient floor,
Footworn and hollowed and thin,
Here was the former door
Where the dead feet walked in.

She sat here in her chair,
Smiling into the fire;
He who played stood there,
Bowing it higher and higher.

Childlike, I danced in a dream;
Blessings emblazoned that day;
Everything glowed with a gleam;
Yet we were looking away!

# IN TENEBRIS

## I

'Percussus sum sicut foenum, et aruit cor meum.' – Ps. ci

Wintertime nighs;
But my bereavement-pain
It cannot bring again:
Twice no one dies.

Flower-petals flee;
But, since it once hath been,
No more that severing scene
Can harrow me.

Birds faint in dread:
I shall not lose old strength
In the lone frost's black length:
Strength long since fled!

Leaves freeze to dun;
But friends can not turn cold
This season as of old
For him with none.

Tempests may scath;
But love can not make smart
Again this year his heart
Who no heart hath.

Black is night's cope;
But death will not appal
One who, past doubtings all,
Waits in unhope.

## IN TENEBRIS

### II

'Considerabam ad dexteram, et videbam; et non erat qui cognosceret
me. . . . Non est qui requirat animam meam.' – Ps. cxli

When the clouds' swoln bosoms echo back the shouts of the
many and strong
That things are all as they best may be, save a few to be right
ere long,
And my eyes have not the vision in them to discern what to
these is so clear,
The blot seems straightway in me alone; one better he were
not here.

The stout upstanders say, All's well with us: ruers have
nought to rue!
And what the potent say so oft, can it fail to be somewhat
true?
Breezily go they, breezily come; their dust smokes around
their career,
Till I think I am one born out of due time, who has no
calling here.

Their dawns bring lusty joys, it seems; their evenings all that
    is sweet;
Our times are blessed times, they cry: Life shapes it as is most
    meet,
And nothing is much the matter; there are many smiles to a
    tear;
Then what is the matter is I, I say. Why should such an one
    be here? . . .

Let him in whose ears the low-voiced Best is killed by the
    clash of the First,
Who holds that if way to the Better there be, it exacts a full
    look at the Worst,
Who feels that delight is a delicate growth cramped by
    crookedness, custom, and fear,
Get him up and be gone as one shaped awry; he disturbs the
    order here.

*1895-6*

# IN TENEBRIS

### III

'Heu mihi, quia incolatus meus prolongatus est! Habitavi cum
habitantibus Cedar; multum incola fuit anima mea.' – Ps. cxix

There have been times when I well might have passed and
    the ending have come –
Points in my path when the dark might have stolen on me,
    artless, unrueing –
Ere I had learnt that the world was a welter of futile
    doing:
Such had been times when I well might have passed, and
    the ending have come!

Say, on the noon when the half-sunny hours told that April
    was nigh,
And I upgathered and cast forth the snow from the crocus-
    border,
Fashioned and furbished the soil into a summer-seeming
    order,
Glowing in gladsome faith that I quickened the year thereby.

Or on that loneliest of eves when afar and benighted we
    stood,
She who upheld me and I, in the midmost of Egdon together,
Confident I in her watching and ward through the
    blackening heather,
Deeming her matchless in might and with measureless scope
    endued.

Or on that winter-wild night when, reclined by the chimney-
    nook quoin,
Slowly a drowse overgat me, the smallest and feeblest of folk
    there,
Weak from my baptism of pain; when at times and anon I
    awoke there –
Heard of a world wheeling on, with no listing or longing to
    join.

Even then! while unweeting that vision could vex or that
    knowledge could numb,
That sweets to the mouth in the belly are bitter, and tart,
    and untoward,
Then, on some dim-coloured scene should my briefly raised
    curtain have lowered,
Then might the Voice that is law have said 'Cease!' and the
    ending have come.

*1896*

## TESS'S LAMENT

### I

I would that folk forgot me quite,
        Forgot me quite!
I would that I could shrink from sight,
    And no more see the sun.
Would it were time to say farewell,
To claim my nook, to need my knell,
Time for them all to stand and tell
    Of my day's work as done

### II

Ah! dairy where I lived so long,
        I lived so long;
Where I would rise up staunch and strong,
    And lie down hopefully.
'Twas there within the chimney-seat
He watched me to the clock's slow beat –
Loved me, and learnt to call me Sweet,
    And whispered words to me.

### III

And now he's gone; and now he's gone; . . .
        And now he's gone!
The flowers we potted perhaps are thrown
    To rot upon the farm.
And where we had our supper-fire
May now grow nettle, dock, and briar,
And all the place be mould and mire
    So cozy once and warm.

### IV

And it was I who did it all,
        Who did it all;
'Twas I who made the blow to fall
    On him who thought no guile.

Well, it is finished – past, and he
Has left me to my misery,
And I must take my Cross on me
     For wronging him awhile.


### v

How gay we looked that day we wed,
           That day we wed!
'May joy be with ye!' they all said
     A-standing by the durn.
I wonder what they say o' us now,
And if they know my lot; and how
She feels who milks my favourite cow,
     And takes my place at churn!


### vi

It wears me out to think of it,
           To think of it;
I cannot bear my fate as writ,
     I'd have my life unbe;
Would turn my memory to a blot,
Make every relic of me rot,
My doings be as they were not,
     And gone all trace of me!

# 3

*from*

## TIME'S LAUGHINGSTOCKS AND OTHER VERSES

# A TRAMPWOMAN'S TRAGEDY
## (182–)

### I

From Wynyard's Gap the livelong day
    The livelong day,
We beat afoot the northward way
    We had travelled times before.
The sun-blaze burning on our backs,
Our shoulders sticking to our packs,
By fosseway, fields, and turnpike tracks
    We skirted sad Sedge-Moor.

### II

Full twenty miles we jaunted on,
    We jaunted on, –
My fancy-man, and jeering John,
    And Mother Lee, and I.
And, as the sun drew down to west,
We climbed the toilsome Poldon crest,
And saw, of landskip sights the best,
    The inn that beamed thereby.

### III

For months we had padded side by side,
    Ay, side by side
Through the Great Forest, Blackmoor wide,
    And where the Parret ran.
We'd faced the gusts on Mendip ridge,
Had crossed the Yeo unhelped by bridge,
Been stung by every Marshwood midge,
    I and my fancy-man.

IV

Lone inns we loved, my man and I,
    My man and I;
'King's Stag', 'Windwhistle' high and dry,
    'The Horse' on Hintock Green,
The cosy house at Wynyard's Gap,
'The Hut' renowned on Bredy Knap,
And many another wayside tap
    Where folk might sit unseen.

V

Now as we trudged – O deadly day,
    O deadly day! –
I teased my fancy-man in play
    And wanton idleness.
I walked alongside jeering John,
I laid his hand my waist upon;
I would not bend my glances on
    My lover's dark distress.

VI

Thus Poldon top at last we won,
    At last we won,
And gained the inn at sink of sun
    Far-famed as 'Marshal's Elm'.
Beneath us figured tor and lea,
From Mendip to the western sea –
I doubt if finer sight there be
    Within this royal realm.

VII

Inside the settle all a-row –
    All four a-row
We sat, I next to John, to show
    That he had wooed and won.
And then he took me on his knee,
And swore it was his turn to be
My favoured mate, and Mother Lee
    Passed to my former one.

VIII

Then in a voice I had never heard,
    I had never heard,
My only Love to me: 'One word,
    My lady, if you please!
Whose is the child you are like to bear? –
*His?* After all my months o' care?'
God knows 'twas not! But, O despair!
    I nodded – still to tease.

IX

Then up he sprung, and with his knife –
    And with his knife
He let out jeering Johnny's life,
    Yes; there, at set of sun.
The slant ray through the window nigh
Gilded John's blood and glazing eye,
Ere scarcely Mother Lee and I
    Knew that the deed was done.

X

The taverns tell the gloomy tale,
    The gloomy tale,
How that at Ivel-chester jail
    My Love, my sweetheart swung;
Though stained till now by no misdeed
Save one horse ta'en in time o' need;
(Blue Jimmy stole right many a steed
    Ere his last fling he flung).

XI

Thereaft I walked the world alone,
    Alone, alone!
On his death-day I gave my groan

And dropt his dead-born child.
'Twas nigh the jail, beneath a tree,
None tending me; for Mother Lee
Had died at Glaston, leaving me
    Unfriended on the wild.

### XII

And in the night as I lay weak,
    As I lay weak,
The leaves a-falling on my cheek,
    The red moon low declined –
The ghost of him I'd die to kiss
Rose up and said: 'Ah, tell me this!
Was the child mine, or was it his?
    Speak, that I rest may find!'

### XIII

O doubt not but I told him then,
    I told him then,
That I had kept me from all men
    Since we joined lips and swore.
Whereat he smiled, and thinned away
As the wind stirred to call up day . . .
– 'Tis past! And here alone I stray
    Haunting the Western Moor.[1]

*April 1902*

1 'Windwhistle' (Stanza IV). The highness and dryness of Windwhistle Inn was impressed upon the writer two or three years ago, when, after climbing on a hot afternoon to the beautiful spot near which it stands and entering the inn for tea, he was informed by the landlady that none could be had, unless he would fetch water from a valley half a mile off, the house containing not a drop, owing to its situation. However, a tantalizing row of full barrels behind her back testified to a wetness of a certain sort, which was not at that time desired.

'Marshal's Elm' (Stanza VI), so picturesquely situated, is no longer an inn, though the house, or part of it, still remains. It used to exhibit a fine old swinging sign.

'Blue Jimmy' (Stanza X) was a notorious horse-stealer of Wessex in those days, who appropriated more than a hundred horses before he

## THE HOUSE OF HOSPITALITIES

Here we broached the Christmas barrel,
    Pushed up the charred log-ends;
Here we sang the Christmas carol,
        And called in friends.

Time has tired me since we met here
    When the folk now dead were young
Since the viands were outset here
        And quaint songs sung.

And the worm has bored the viol
    That used to lead the tune,
Rust eaten out the dial
        That struck night's noon.

Now no Christmas brings in neighbours,
    And the New Year comes unlit;
Where we sang the mole now labours,
        And spiders knit.

Yet at midnight if here walking,
    When the moon sheets wall and tree,
I see forms of old time talking,
        Who smile on me.

was caught, among others one belonging to a neighbour of the writer's
randfather. He was hanged at the now demolished Ivel-chester or
chester jail above mentioned – that building formerly of so many
nister associations in the minds of the local peasantry, and the con-
nual haunt of fever, which at last led to its condemnation. Its site is
ow an innocent-looking green meadow.

# THE CURATE'S KINDNESS

## A WORKHOUSE IRONY

### I

I thought they'd be strangers aroun' me,
    But she's to be there!
Let me jump out o' waggon and go back and drown me
    At Pummery or Ten-Hatches Weir.

### II

I thought: 'Well, I've come to the Union –
    The workhouse at last –
After honest hard work all the week, and Communion
    O' Zundays, these fifty years past.

### III

' 'Tis hard; but', I thought, 'never mind it:
    There's gain in the end:
And when I get used to the place I shall find it
    A home, and may find there a friend.

### IV

'Life there will be better than t'other,
    For peace is assured.
*The men in one wing and their wives in another*
    Is strictly the rule of the Board.'

### V

Just then one young Pa'son arriving
    Steps up out of breath
To the side o' the waggon wherein we were driving
    To Union; and calls out and saith:

VI

Old folks, that harsh order is altered,
    Be not sick of heart!
The Guardians they poohed and they pished and they paltered
    When urged not to keep you apart.

VII

"It is wrong", I maintained, "to divide them,
    Near forty years wed."
Very well, sir. We promise, then, they shall abide them
    In one wing together", they said.'

VIII

Then I sank – knew 'twas quite a foredone thing
    That misery should be
To the end! . . . To get freed of her there was the one thing
    Had made the change welcome to me.

IX

To go there was ending but badly;
    'Twas shame and 'twas pain;
But anyhow', thought I, 'thereby I shall gladly
    Get free of this forty years' chain.'

X

I thought they'd be strangers aroun' me,
    But she's to be there!
Let me jump out o' waggon and go back and drown me
    At Pummery or Ten-Hatches Weir.

# THE FARM-WOMAN'S WINTER

### I

If seasons all were summers,
    And leaves would never fall,
And hopping casement-comers
    Were foodless not at all,
And fragile folk might be here
    That white winds bid depart;
Then one I used to see here
    Would warm my wasted heart!

### II

One frail, who, bravely tilling
    Long hours in gripping gusts,
Was mastered by their chilling,
    And now his ploughshare rusts.
So savage winter catches
    The breath of limber things,
And what I love he snatches,
    And what I love not, brings.

# SHUT OUT THAT MOON

Close up the casement, draw the blind,
    Shut out that stealing moon,
She wears too much the guise she wore
    Before our lutes were strewn
With years-deep dust, and names we read
    On a white stone were hewn.

Step not forth on the dew-dashed lawn
    To view the Lady's Chair,
Immense Orion's glittering form,
    The Less and Greater Bear:

Stay in; to such sights we were drawn
    When faded ones were fair.

Brush not the bough for midnight scents
    That come forth lingeringly,
And wake the same sweet sentiments
    They breathed to you and me
When living seemed a laugh, and love
    All it was said to be.

Within the common lamp-lit room
    Prison my eyes and thought;
Let dingy details crudely loom,
    Mechanic speech be wrought:
Too fragrant was Life's early bloom,
    Too tart the fruit it brought!

*1904*

# THE DIVISION

Rain on the windows, creaking doors,
    With blasts that besom the green,
And I am here, and you are there,
    And a hundred miles between!

O were it but the weather, Dear,
    O were it but the miles
That summed up all our severance,
    There might be room for smiles.

But that thwart thing betwixt us twain,
    Which nothing cleaves or clears,
Is more than distance, Dear, or rain,
    And longer than the years!

*1893*

# ON THE DEPARTURE PLATFORM

We kissed at the barrier; and passing through
She left me, and moment by moment got
Smaller and smaller, until to my view
    She was but a spot;

A wee white spot of muslin fluff
That down the diminishing platform bore
Through hustling crowds of gentle and rough
    To the carriage door.

Under the lamplight's fitful glowers,
Behind dark groups from far and near,
Whose interests were apart from ours,
    She would disappear,

Then show again, till I ceased to see
That flexible form, that nebulous white;
And she who was more than my life to me
    Had vanished quite. . . .

We have penned new plans since that fair fond day,
And in season she will appear again –
Perhaps in the same soft white array –
    But never as then!

– 'And why, young man, must eternally fly
A joy you'll repeat, if you love her well?'
– O friend, nought happens twice thus; why,
    I cannot tell!

## 'I SAY I'LL SEEK HER'

I say, 'I'll seek her side
    Ere hindrance interposes';
    But eve in midnight closes,
And here I still abide.

When darkness wears I see
　　Her sad eyes in a vision;
　　They ask, 'What indecision
Detains you, Love, from me? –

'The creaking hinge is oiled,
　　I have unbarred the backway,
　　But you tread not the trackway
And shall the thing be spoiled?

'Far cockcrows echo shrill,
　　The shadows are abating,
　　And I am waiting, waiting;
But O, you tarry still!'

# THE END OF THE EPISODE

　　Indulge no more may we
In this sweet-bitter pastime:
The love-light shines the last time
　　Between you, Dear, and me.

　　There shall remain no trace
Of what so closely tied us,
And blank as ere love eyed us
　　Will be our meeting-place.

　　The flowers and thymy air,
Will they now miss our coming?
The dumbles thin their humming
　　To find we haunt not there?

　　Though fervent was our vow,
Though ruddily ran our pleasure,
Bliss has fulfilled its measure,
　　And sees its sentence now.

Ache deep; but make no moans:
Smile out; but stilly suffer:
The paths of love are rougher
Than thoroughfares of stones.


# AT CASTERBRIDGE FAIR

## II

### FORMER BEAUTIES

These market-dames, mid-aged, with lips thin-drawn,
And tissues sere,
Are they the ones we loved in years agone,
And courted here?

Are these the muslined pink young things to whom
We vowed and swore
In nooks on summer Sundays by the Froom,
Or Budmouth shore?

Do they remember those gay tunes we trod
Clasped on the green;
Aye; trod till moonlight set on the beaten sod
A satin sheen?

They must forget, forget! They cannot know
What once they were,
Or memory would transfigure them, and show
Them always fair.


## IV

### THE MARKET-GIRL

Nobody took any notice of her as she stood on the causey
kerb,
All eager to sell her honey and apples and bunches of garden
herb;

And if she had offered to give her wares and herself with them
    too that day,
I doubt if a soul would have cared to take a bargain so choice
    away.

But chancing to trace her sunburnt grace that morning as I
    passed nigh,
I went and I said 'Poor maidy dear! – and will none of the
    people buy?'
And so it began; and soon we knew what the end of it all
    must be,
And I found that though no others had bid, a prize had been
    won by me.

## VI

### A WIFE WAITS

Will's at the dance in the Club-room below,
    Where the tall liquor-cups foam;
I on the pavement up here by the Bow,[1]
    Wait, wait, to steady him home.

Will and his partner are treading a tune,
    Loving companions they be;
Willy, before we were married in June,
    Said he loved no one but me;

Said he would let his old pleasures all go
    Ever to live with his Dear.
Will's at the dance in the Club-room below,
    Shivering I wait for him here.

[1] The old name for the curved corner by the cross-streets in the
middle of Casterbridge.

# THE DARK-EYED GENTLEMAN

### I

I pitched my day's leazings[1] in Crimmercrock Lane,
To tie up my garter and jog on again,
When a dear dark-eyed gentleman passed there and said,
In a way that made all o' me colour rose-red,
    'What do I see –
    O pretty knee!'
And he came and he tied up my garter for me.

### II

'Twixt sunset and moonrise it was, I can mind:
Ah, 'tis easy to lose what we nevermore find! –
Of the dear stranger's home, of his name, I knew nought,
But I soon knew his nature and all that it brought.
    Then bitterly
    Sobbed I that he
Should ever have tied up my garter for me!

### III

Yet now I've beside me a fine lissom lad,
And my slip's nigh forgot, and my days are not sad;
My own dearest joy is he, comrade, and friend,
He it is who safe-guards me, on him I depend;
    No sorrow brings he,
    And thankful I be
That his daddy once tied up my garter for me!

[1] Bundle of gleaned corn.

## A DREAM QUESTION

'It shall be dark unto you, that ye shall not divine.' – Micah III:

I asked the Lord: 'Sire, is this true
Which hosts of theologians hold,
That when we creatures censure you
For shaping griefs and ails untold
(Deeming them punishments undue)
You rage, as Moses wrote of old?

'When we exclaim: "Beneficent
He is not, for he orders pain,
Or, if so, not omnipotent:
To a mere child the thing is plain!"
Those who profess to represent
You, cry out: "Impious and profane!" '

He: 'Save me from my friends, who deem
That I care what my creatures say!
Mouth as you list: sneer, rail, blaspheme,
O manikin, the livelong day,
Not one grief-groan or pleasure-gleam
Will you increase or take away.

'Why things are thus, whoso derides,
May well remain my secret still . . . .
A fourth dimension, say the guides,
To matter is conceivable.
Think some such mystery resides
Within the ethic of my will.'

## THE RAMBLER

I do not see the hills around,
Nor mark the tints the copses wear;
I do not note the grassy ground
And constellated daisies there.

I hear not the contralto note
Of cuckoos hid on either hand,
The whirr that shakes the nighthawk's throat
When eve's brown awning hoods the land.

Some say each songster, tree, and mead –
All eloquent of love divine –
Receives their constant careful heed:
Such keen appraisement is not mine.

The tones around me that I hear,
The aspects, meanings, shapes I see,
Are those far back ones missed when near,
And now perceived too late by me!

# THE PINE PLANTERS

## (MARTY SOUTH'S REVERIE)

### I

We work here together
    In blast and breeze;
He fills the earth in,
    I hold the trees.

He does not notice
    That what I do
Keeps me from moving
    And chills me through.

He has seen one fairer
    I feel by his eye,
Which skims me as though
    I were not by.

And since she passed here
    He scarce has known
But that the woodland
    Holds him alone.

I have worked here with him
　　Since morning shine,
He busy with his thoughts
　　And I with mine.

I have helped him so many,
　　So many days,
But never win any
　　Small word of praise!

Shall I not sigh to him
　　That I work on
Glad to be nigh to him
　　Though hope is gone?

Nay, though he never
　　Knew love like mine,
I'll bear it ever
　　And make no sign!


II

From the bundle at hand here
　　I take each tree,
And set it to stand, here
　　Always to be;
When, in a second,
　　As if from fear
Of Life unreckoned
　　Beginning here,
It starts a sighing
　　Through day and night,
Though while there lying
　　'Twas voiceless quite.

It will sigh in the morning,
　　Will sigh at noon,
At the winter's warning,
　　In wafts of June;

Grieving that never
    Kind Fate decreed
It should for ever
    Remain a seed,
And shun the welter
    Of things without,
Unneeding shelter
    From storm and drought.

Thus, all unknowing
    For whom or what
We set it growing
    In this bleak spot,
It still will grieve here
    Throughout its time,
Unable to leave here,
    Or change its clime:
Or tell the story
    Of us today
When, halt and hoary,
    We pass away.

## SHE HEARS THE STORM

There was a time in former years –
    While my roof-tree was his –
When I should have been distressed by fears
    At such a night as this!

I should have murmured anxiously,
    'The pricking rain strikes cold;
His road is bare of hedge or tree,
    And he is getting old.'

But now the fitful chimney-roar,
    The drone of Thorncombe trees,
The Froom in flood upon the moor,
    The mud of Mellstock Leaze,

The candle slanting sooty wick'd,
    The thuds upon the thatch,
The eaves-drops on the window flicked,
    The clacking garden-hatch,

And what they mean to wayfarers,
    I scarcely heed or mind;
He has won that storm-tight roof of hers
    Which Earth grants all her kind.

# NEW YEAR'S EVE

'I have finished another year', said God,
    'In grey, green, white, and brown;
I have strewn the leaf upon the sod,
Sealed up the worm within the clod,
    And let the last sun down.'

'And what's the good of it?' I said,
    'What reasons made you call
From formless void this earth we tread,
When nine-and-ninety can be read
    Why nought should be at all?

'Yea, Sire; why shaped you us, "who in
    This tabernacle groan" –
If ever a joy be found herein,
Such joy no man had wished to win
    If he had never known!'

Then he: 'My labours – logicless –
    You may explain; not I:
Sense-sealed I have wrought, without a guess
That I evolved a Consciousness
    To ask for reasons why.

'Strange that ephemeral creatures who
    By my own ordering are,
Should see the shortness of my view,
Use ethic tests I never knew,
    Or made provision for!'

He sank to raptness as of yore,
    And opening New Year's Day
Wove it by rote as theretofore,
And went on working evermore
    In his unweeting way.

1906

# THE MAN HE KILLED

'Had he and I but met
    By some old ancient inn,
We should have sat us down to wet
    Right many a nipperkin!

'But ranged as infantry,
    And staring face to face,
I shot at him as he at me,
    And killed him in his place.

'I shot him dead because –
    Because he was my foe,
Just so: my foe of course he was;
    That's clear enough; although

'He thought he'd 'list, perhaps,
    Off-hand like – just as I –
Was out of work – had sold his traps –
    No other reason why.

'Yes; quaint and curious war is!
    You shoot a fellow down
You'd treat if met where any bar is,
    Or help to half a crown.'

1902

# 4

*from*

SATIRES OF CIRCUMSTANCE
LYRICS AND REVERIES

# CHANNEL FIRING

That night your great guns, unawares,
Shook all our coffins as we lay,
And broke the chancel window-squares,
We thought it was the Judgement-day

And sat upright. While drearisome
Arose the howl of wakened hounds:
The mouse let fall the altar-crumb,
The worms drew back into the mounds,

The glebe cow drooled. Till God called, 'No;
It's gunnery practice out at sea
Just as before you went below;
The world is as it used to be:

'All nations striving strong to make
Red war yet redder. Mad as hatters
They do no more for Christés sake
Than you who are helpless in such matters.

'That this is not the judgement-hour
For some of them's a blessed thing,
For if it were they'd have to scour
Hell's floor for so much threatening. . . .

'Ha, ha. It will be warmer when
I blow the trumpet (if indeed
I ever do; for you are men,
And rest eternal sorely need).'

So down we lay again. 'I wonder,
Will the world ever saner be',
Said one, 'than when He sent us under
In our indifferent century!'

And many a skeleton shook his head.
'Instead of preaching forty year',
My neighbour Parson Thirdly said,
'I wish I had stuck to pipes and beer.'

Again the guns disturbed the hour,
Roaring their readiness to avenge,
As far inland as Stourton Tower,
And Camelot, and starlit Stonehenge.

*April 1914*

# THE CONVERGENCE OF THE TWAIN

## (*Lines on the loss of the* Titanic)

### I

In a solitude of the sea
Deep from human vanity,
And the Pride of Life that planned her, stilly couches she.

### II

Steel chambers, late the pyres
Of her salamandrine fires,
Cold currents thrid, and turn to rhythmic tidal lyres.

### III

Over the mirrors meant
To glass the opulent
The sea-worm crawls – grotesque, slimed, dumb, indifferent.

### IV

Jewels in joy designed
To ravish the sensuous mind
Lie lightless, all their sparkles bleared and black and blind.

V

Dim moon-eyed fishes near
Gaze at the gilded gear
And query: 'What does this vaingloriousness down here?'


VI

Well: while was fashioning
This creature of cleaving wing,
The Immanent Will that stirs and urges everything


VII

Prepared a sinister mate
For her – so gaily great –
A Shape of Ice, for the time far and dissociate.


VIII

And as the smart ship grew
In stature, grace, and hue,
In shadowy silent distance grew the Iceberg too.


IX

Alien they seemed to be:
No mortal eye could see
The intimate welding of their later history,


X

Or sign that they were bent
By paths coincident
On being anon twin halves of one august event.


XI

Till the Spinner of the Years
Said 'Now!' And each one hears,
And consummation comes, and jars two hemispheres.

# AFTER THE VISIT

## (*To F. E. D.*)

Come again to the place
Where your presence was as a leaf that skims
Down a drouthy way whose ascent bedims
The bloom on the farer's face.

Come again, with the feet
That were light on the green as a thistledown ball,
And those mute ministrations to one and to all
Beyond a man's saying sweet.

Until then the faint scent
Of the bordering flowers swam unheeded away,
And I marked not the charm in the changes of day
As the cloud-colours came and went.

Through the dark corridors
Your walk was so soundless I did not know
Your form from a phantom's of long ago
Said to pass on the ancient floors,

Till you drew from the shade,
And I saw the large luminous living eyes
Regard me in fixed inquiring-wise
As those of a soul that weighed,

Scarce consciously,
The eternal question of what Life was,
And why we were there, and by whose strange laws
That which mattered most could not be.

# 'WHEN I SET OUT FOR LYONNESSE'
## (1870)

When I set out for Lyonnesse,
 A hundred miles away,
 The rime was on the spray,
And starlight lit my lonesomeness
When I set out for Lyonnesse
 A hundred miles away.

What would bechance at Lyonnesse
 While I should sojourn there
 No prophet durst declare,
Nor did the wisest wizard guess
What would bechance at Lyonnesse
 While I should sojourn there.

When I came back from Lyonnesse
 With magic in my eyes,
 All marked with mute surmise
My radiance rare and fathomless,
When I came back from Lyonnesse
 With magic in my eyes!

*1870*

# THE FACE AT THE CASEMENT

 If ever joy leave
An abiding sting of sorrow,
So befell it on the morrow
 Of that May eve. . . .

 The travelled sun dropped
To the north-west, low and lower,
The pony's trot grew slower,
 Until we stopped.

'This cosy house just by
I must call at for a minute,
A sick man lies within it
    Who soon will die.

'He wished to – marry me,
So I am bound, when I drive near him,
To inquire, if but to cheer him,
    How he may be.'

A message was sent in,
And wordlessly we waited,
Till some one came and stated
    The bulletin.

And that the sufferer said,
For her call no words could thank her;
As his angel he must rank her
    Till life's spark fled.

Slowly we drove away,
When I turned my head, although not
Called to: why I turned I know not
    Even to this day:

And lo, there in my view
Pressed against an upper lattice
Was a white face, gazing at us
    As we withdrew.

And well did I divine
It to be the man's there dying,
Who but lately had been sighing
    For her pledged mine.

Then I deigned a deed of hell;
It was done before I knew it;
What devil made me do it
    I cannot tell!

Yes, while he gazed above,
I put my arm about her
That he might see, nor doubt her
   My plighted Love.

The pale face vanished quick,
As if blasted, from the casement,
And my shame and self-abasement
   Began their prick.

And they prick on, ceaselessly,
For that stab in Love's fierce fashion
Which, unfired by lover's passion,
   Was foreign to me.

She smiled at my caress,
But why came the soft embowment
Of her shoulder at that moment
   She did not guess.

Long long years has he lain
In thy garth, O sad Saint Cleather:
What tears there, bared to weather,
   Will cleanse that stain!

Love is long-suffering, brave,
Sweet, prompt, precious as a jewel;
But jealousy is cruel,
   Cruel as the grave!

# WESSEX HEIGHTS

## (1896)

There are some heights in Wessex, shaped as if by a kindly
    hand
For thinking, dreaming, dying on, and at crises when I stand,
Say, on Ingpen Beacon eastward, or on Wylls-Neck west-
    wardly,
I seem where I was before my birth, and after death may be.

In the lowlands I have no comrade, not even the lone man's
    friend –
Her who suffereth long and is kind; accepts what he is too
    weak to mend:
Down there they are dubious and askance; there nobody
    thinks as I,
But mind-chains do not clank where one's next neighbour is
    the sky.

In the towns I am tracked by phantoms having weird detective
    ways –
Shadows of beings who fellowed with myself of earlier days:
They hang about at places, and they say harsh heavy things –
Men with a wintry sneer, and women with tart disparagings.

Down there I seem to be false to myself, my simple self that
    was,
And is not now, and I see him watching, wondering what
    crass cause
Can have merged him into such a strange continuator as this,
Who yet has something in common with himself, my
    chrysalis.

I cannot go to the great grey Plain; there's a figure against the
    moon,
Nobody sees it but I, and it makes my breast beat out of tune;

I cannot go to the tall-spired town, being barred by the forms
    now passed
For everybody but me, in whose long vision they stand there
    fast.

There's a ghost at Yell'ham Bottom chiding loud at the fall
    of the night,
There's a ghost in Froom-side Vale, thin-lipped and vague,
    in a shroud of white,
There is one in the railway train whenever I do not want it
    near,
I see its profile against the pane, saying what I would not hear.

As for one rare fair woman, I am now but a thought of hers,
I enter her mind and another thought succeeds me that she
    prefers;
Yet my love for her in its fullness she herself even did not
    know;
Well, time cures hearts of tenderness, and now I can let her
    go.

So I am found on Ingpen Beacon, or on Wylls-Neck to the
    west,
Or else on homely Bulbarrow, or little Pilsdon Crest,
Where men have never cared to haunt, nor women have
    walked with me,
And ghosts then keep their distance; and I know some
    liberty.


# A SINGER ASLEEP

## (Algernon Charles Swinburne, 1837–1909)

### I

In this fair niche above the unslumbering sea,
  That sentrys up and down all night, all day,
  From cove to promontory, from ness to bay,
The Fates have fitly bidden that he should be
    Pillowed eternally.

II

– It was as though a garland of red roses
Had fallen about the hood of some smug nun
When irresponsibly dropped as from the sun,
In fulth of numbers freaked with musical closes,
Upon Victoria's formal middle time
     His leaves of rhythm and rhyme.


III

O that far morning of a summer day
When, down a terraced street whose pavements lay
Glassing the sunshine into my bent eyes,
I walked and read with a quick glad surprise
     New words, in classic guise, –


IV

The passionate pages of his earlier years,
Fraught with hot sighs, sad laughters, kisses, tears;
Fresh-fluted notes, yet from a minstrel who
Blew them not naïvely, but as one who knew
     Full well why thus he blew.


V

I still can hear the brabble and the roar
At those thy tunes, O still one, now passed through
That fitful fire of tongues then entered new!
Their power is spent like spindrift on this shore;
     Thine swells yet more and more.


VI

– His singing-mistress verily was no other
Than she the Lesbian, she the music-mother
Of all the tribe that feel in melodies;
Who leapt, love-anguished, from the Leucadian steep
Into the rambling world-encircling deep
     Which hides her where none sees.

VII

And one can hold in thought that nightly here
His phantom may draw down to the water's brim,
And hers come up to meet it, as a dim
Lone shine upon the heaving hydrosphere,
And mariners wonder as they traverse near,
      Unknowing of her and him.

VIII

One dreams him sighing to her spectral form:
'O teacher, where lies hid thy burning line;
Where are those songs, O poetess divine
Whose very orts are love incarnadine?'
And her smile back: 'Disciple true and warm,
      Sufficient now are thine.' . . .

IX

So here, beneath the waking constellations,
Where the waves peal their everlasting strains,
And their dull subterrene reverberations
Shake him when storms make mountains of their plains –
Him once their peer in sad improvisations,
And deft as wind to cleave their frothy manes –
I leave him, while the daylight gleam declines
      Upon the capes and chines.

*Bonchurch, 1910*

# A PLAINT TO MAN

When you slowly emerged from the den of Time,
And gained percipience as you grew,
And fleshed you fair out of shapeless slime,

Wherefore, O Man, did there come to you
The unhappy need of creating me –
A form like your own – for praying to?

My virtue, power, utility,
Within my maker must all abide,
Since none in myself can ever be,

One thin as a phasm on a lantern-slide
Shown forth in the dark upon some dim sheet,
And by none but its showman vivified.

'Such a forced device', you may say, 'is meet
For easing a loaded heart at whiles:
Man needs to conceive of a mercy-seat

'Somewhere above the gloomy aisles
Of this wailful world, or he could not bear
The irk no local hope beguiles.'

– But since I was framed in your first despair
The doing without me has had no play
In the minds of men when shadows scare;

And now that I dwindle day by day
Beneath the deicide eyes of seers
In a light that will not let me stay,

And tomorrow the whole of me disappears,
The truth should be told, and the fact be faced
That had best been faced in earlier years:

The fact of life with dependence placed
On the human heart's resource alone,
In brotherhood bonded close and graced

With loving-kindness fully blown,
And visioned help unsought, unknown.

*1909–10*

# 'AH, ARE YOU DIGGING ON MY GRAVE?'

'Ah, are you digging on my grave,
    My loved one? – planting rue?'
– 'No: yesterday he went to wed
One of the brightest wealth has bred.
"It cannot hurt her now," he said,
    "That I should not be true." '

'Then who is digging on my grave?
    My nearest dearest kin?'
– 'Ah, no: they sit and think, "What use!
What good will planting flowers produce?
No tendance of her mound can loose
    Her spirit from Death's gin." '

'But some one digs upon my grave?
    My enemy? – prodding sly?'
– 'Nay: when she heard you had passed the Gate
That shuts on all flesh soon or late,
She thought you no more worth her hate,
    And cares not where you lie.'

'Then, who is digging on my grave?
    Say – since I have not guessed!'
– 'O it is I, my mistress dear,
Your little dog, who still lives near,
And much I hope my movements here
    Have not disturbed your rest?'

'Ah, yes! *You* dig upon my grave . . .
    Why flashed it not on me
That one true heart was left behind!
What feeling do we ever find
To equal among human kind
    A dog's fidelity!'

'Mistress, I dug upon your grave
    To bury a bone, in case
I should be hungry near this spot
When passing on my daily trot.
I am sorry, but I quite forgot
    It was your resting-place.'


## AT DAY-CLOSE IN NOVEMBER

The ten hours' light is abating
    And a late bird wings across,
Where the pines, like waltzers waiting,
    Give their black heads a toss.

Beech leaves, that yellow the noon-time,
    Float past like specks in the eye;
I set every tree in my June time,
    And now they obscure the sky.

And the children who ramble through here
    Conceive that there never has been
A time when no tall trees grew here,
    That none will in time be seen.


## UNDER THE WATERFALL

'Whenever I plunge my arm, like this,
In a basin of water, I never miss
The sweet sharp sense of a fugitive day
Fetched back from its thickening shroud of gray.
    Hence the only prime
    And real love-rhyme
    That I know by heart,
    And that leaves no smart,

Is the purl of a little valley fall
About three spans wide and two spans tall
Over a table of solid rock,
And into a scoop of the self-same block;
The purl of a runlet that never ceases
In stir of kingdoms, in wars, in peaces;
With a hollow boiling voice it speaks
And has spoken since hills were turfless peaks.'

'And why gives this the only prime
Idea to you of a real love-rhyme?
And why does plunging your arm in a bowl
Full of spring water, bring throbs to your soul?'

'Well, under the fall, in a crease of the stone,
Though where precisely none ever has known,
Jammed darkly, nothing to show how prized,
And by now with its smoothness opalized,

     Is a drinking-glass:
     For, down that pass
     My lover and I
     Walked under a sky

Of blue with a leaf-wove awning of green,
In the burn of August, to paint the scene,
And we placed our basket of fruit and wine
By the runlet's rim, where we sat to dine;
And when we had drunk from the glass together,
Arched by the oak-copse from the weather,
I held the vessel to rinse in the fall,
Where it slipped, and sank, and was past recall,
Though we stooped and plumbed the little abyss
With long bared arms. There the glass still is.
And, as said, if I thrust my arm below
Cold water in basin or bowl, a throe
From the past awakens a sense of that time,
And the glass we used, and the cascade's rhyme.
The basin seems the pool, and its edge
The hard smooth face of the brook-side ledge,

And the leafy pattern of china-ware
The hanging plants that were bathing there.

'By night, by day, when it shines or lours,
There lies intact that chalice of ours,
And its presence adds to the rhyme of love
Persistently sung by the fall above.
No lip has touched it since his and mine
In turns therefrom sipped lovers' wine.'

# THE GOING

Why did you give no hint that night
That quickly after the morrow's dawn,
And calmly, as if indifferent quite,
You would close your term here, up and be gone
    Where I could not follow
    With wing of swallow
To gain one glimpse of you ever anon!

    Never to bid good-bye,
    Or lip me the softest call,
Or utter a wish for a word, while I
Saw morning harden upon the wall,
    Unmoved, unknowing
    That your great going
Had place that moment, and altered all.

Why do you make me leave the house
And think for a breath it is you I see
At the end of the alley of bending boughs
Where so often at dusk you used to be;
    Till in darkening dankness
    The yawning blankness
Of the perspective sickens me!

You were she who abode
By those red-veined rocks far West,
You were the swan-necked one who rode
Along the beetling Beeny Crest,
And, reining nigh me,
Would muse and eye me,
While Life unrolled us its very best.

Why, then, latterly did we not speak,
Did we not think of those days long dead,
And ere your vanishing strive to seek
That time's renewal? We might have said,
'In this bright spring weather
We'll visit together
Those places that once we visited.'

Well, well! All's past amend,
Unchangeable. It must go.
I seem but a dead man held on end
To sink down soon. . . . O you could not know
That such swift fleeing
No soul foreseeing –
Not even I – would undo me so!

*December 1912*


## YOUR LAST DRIVE

Here by the moorway you returned,
And saw the borough lights ahead
That lit your face – all undiscerned
To be in a week the face of the dead,
And you told of the charm of that haloed view
That never again would beam on you.

And on your left you passed the spot
Where eight days later you were to lie,
And be spoken of as one who was not;
Beholding it with a heedless eye
As alien from you, though under its tree
You soon would halt everlastingly.

I drove not with you. . . . Yet had I sat
At your side that eve I should not have seen
That the countenance I was glancing at
Had a last-time look in the flickering sheen,
Nor have read the writing upon your face,
'I go hence soon to my resting-place;

'You may miss me then. But I shall not know
How many times you visit me there,
Or what your thoughts are, or if you go
There never at all. And I shall not care.
Should you censure me I shall take no heed,
And even your praises no more shall need.'

True: never you'll know. And you will not mind.
But shall I then slight you because of such?
Dear ghost, in the past did you ever find
The thought 'What profit' move me much?
Yet abides the fact, indeed, the same, –
You are past love, praise, indifference, blame.

*December 1912*


## 'I FOUND HER OUT THERE'

I found her out there
On a slope few see,
That falls westwardly
To the salt-edged air,

Where the ocean breaks
On the purple strand,
And the hurricane shakes
The solid land.

I brought her here,
And have laid her to rest
In a noiseless nest
No sea beats near.
She will never be stirred
In her loamy cell
By the waves long heard
And loved so well.

So she does not sleep
By those haunted heights
The Atlantic smites
And the blind gales sweep,
Whence she often would gaze
At Dundagel's famed head,
While the dipping blaze
Dyed her face fire-red;

And would sigh at the tale
Of sunk Lyonnesse,
As a wind-tugged tress
Flapped her cheek like a flail;
Or listen at whiles
With a thought-bound brow
To the murmuring miles
She is far from now.

Yet her shade, maybe,
Will creep underground
Till it catch the sound
Of that western sea
As it swells and sobs
Where she once domiciled,
And joy in its throbs
With the heart of a child.

# LAMENT

How she would have loved
A party today! –
Bright-hatted and gloved,
With table and tray
And chairs on the lawn
Her smiles would have shone
With welcomings. . . . But
She is shut, she is shut
　　From friendship's spell
　　In the jailing shell
　　Of her tiny cell.

Or she would have reigned
At a dinner tonight
With ardours unfeigned,
And a generous delight;
All in her abode
She'd have freely bestowed
On her guests. . . . But alas,
She is shut under grass
　　Where no cups flow,
　　Powerless to know
　　That it might be so.

And she would have sought
With a child's eager glance
The shy snowdrops brought
By the new year's advance,
And peered in the rime
Of Candlemas-time
For crocuses . . . chanced
It that she were not tranced
　　From sights she loved best;
　　Wholly possessed
　　By an infinite rest!

And we are here staying
Amid these stale things,
Who care not for gaying,
And those junketings
That used so to joy her,
And never to cloy her
As us they cloy! . . . But
She is shut, she is shut
  From the cheer of them, dead
  To all done and said
  In her yew-arched bed.


# THE HAUNTER

He does not think that I haunt here nightly
  How shall I let him know
That whither his fancy sets him wandering
  I, too, alertly go? –
Hover and hover a few feet from him
  Just as I used to do,
But cannot answer the words he lifts me –
  Only listen thereto!

When I could answer he did not say them:
  When I could let him know
How I would like to join in his journeys
  Seldom he wished to go.
Now that he goes and wants me with him
  More than he used to do,
Never he sees my faithful phantom
  Though he speaks thereto.

Yes, I companion him to places
  Only dreamers know,
Where the shy hares print long paces,
  Where the night rooks go;

Into old aisles where the past is all to him,
  Close as his shade can do,
Always lacking the power to call to him,
  Near as I reach thereto!

What a good haunter I am, O tell him!
  Quickly make him know
If he but sigh since my loss befell him
  Straight to his side I go.
Tell him a faithful one is doing
  All that love can do
Still that his path may be worth pursuing,
  And to bring peace thereto.


# THE VOICE

Woman much missed, how you call to me, call to me,
Saying that now you are not as you were
When you had changed from the one who was all to me,
But as at first, when our day was fair.

Can it be you that I hear? Let me view you, then,
Standing as when I drew near to the town
Where you would wait for me: yes, as I knew you then,
Even to the original air-blue gown!

Or is it only the breeze, in its listlessness
Travelling across the wet mead to me here,
You being ever dissolved to wan wistlessness,
Heard no more again far or near?

  Thus I; faltering forward,
    Leaves around me falling,
Wind oozing thin through the thorn from norward,
    And the woman calling.

*December 1912*

## AFTER A JOURNEY

Hereto I come to view a voiceless ghost;
    Whither, O whither will its whim now draw me?
Up the cliff, down, till I'm lonely, lost,
    And the unseen waters' ejaculations awe me.
Where you will next be there's no knowing,
    Facing round about me everywhere,
        With your nut-coloured hair,
And gray eyes, and rose-flush coming and going.

Yes: I have re-entered your olden haunts at last;
    Through the years, through the dead scenes I have tracked
        you;
What have you now found to say of our past –
    Scanned across the dark space wherein I have lacked you?
Summer gave us sweets, but autumn wrought division?
    Things were not lastly as firstly well
        With us twain, you tell?
But all's closed now, despite Time's derision.

I see what you are doing: you are leading me on
    To the spots we knew when we haunted here together,
The waterfall, above which the mist-bow shone
    At the then fair hour in the then fair weather,
And the cave just under, with a voice still so hollow
    That it seems to call out to me from forty years ago,
        When you were all aglow,
And not the thin ghost that I now frailly follow!

Ignorant of what there is flitting here to see,
    The waked birds preen and the seals flop lazily;
Soon you will have, Dear, to vanish from me,
    For the stars close their shutters and the dawn whitens
        hazily.

Trust me, I mind not, though Life lours,
  The bringing me here; nay, bring me here again!
      I am just the same as when
Our days were a joy, and our paths through flowers.

   *Pentargan Bay*


# BEENY CLIFF

## *March 1870 – March 1913*


### I

O the opal and the sapphire of that wandering western sea,
And the woman riding high above with bright hair flapping
    free –
The woman whom I loved so, and who loyally loved me.


### II

The pale mews plained below us, and the waves seemed far
    away
In a nether sky, engrossed in saying their ceaseless babbling
    say,
As we laughed light-heartedly aloft on that clear-sunned
    March day.


### III

A little cloud then cloaked us, and there flew an irised rain,
And the Atlantic dyed its levels with a dull misfeatured stain,
And then the sun burst out again, and purples prinked the
    main.


### IV

– Still in all its chasmal beauty bulks old Beeny to the sky,
And shall she and I not go there once again now March is
    nigh,
And the sweet things said in that March say anew there by
    and by?

V

What if still in chasmal beauty looms that wild weird
    western shore,
The woman now is – elsewhere – whom the ambling pony
    bore,
And nor knows nor cares for Beeny, and will laugh there
    nevermore.


# AT CASTLE BOTEREL

As I drive to the junction of lane and highway,
    And the drizzle bedrenches the waggonette,
I look behind at the fading byway,
    And see on its slope, now glistening wet,
        Distinctly yet

Myself and a girlish form benighted
    In dry March weather. We climb the road
Beside a chaise. We had just alighted
    To ease the sturdy pony's load
        When he sighed and slowed.

What we did as we climbed, and what we talked of
    Matters not much, nor to what it led, –
Something that life will not be balked of
    Without rude reason till hope is dead,
        And feeling fled.

It filled but a minute. But was there ever
    A time of such quality, since or before,
In that hill's story? To one mind never,
    Though it has been climbed, foot-swift, foot-sore,
        By thousands more.

Primeval rocks form the road's steep border,
    And much have they faced there, first and last,
Of the transitory in Earth's long order;
    But what they record in colour and cast
        Is – that we two passed.

And to me, though Time's unflinching rigour,
  In mindless rote, has ruled from sight
The substance now, one phantom figure
  Remains on the slope, as when that night
    Saw us alight.

I look and see it there, shrinking, shrinking,
  I look back at it amid the rain
For the very last time; for my sand is sinking,
  And I shall traverse old love's domain
    Never again.

*March 1913*

# THE PHANTOM HORSEWOMAN

### I

Queer are the ways of a man I know:
      He comes and stands
      In a careworn craze,
      And looks at the sands
      And the seaward haze
      With moveless hands
      And face and gaze,
      Then turns to go . . .
And what does he see when he gazes so?

### II

They say he sees as an instant thing
      More clear than today,
      A sweet soft scene
      That was once in play
      By that briny green;
      Yes, notes alway
      Warm, real, and keen,
      What his back years bring –
A phantom of his own figuring.

### III

Of this vision of his they might say more:
      Not only there
      Does he see this sight,
      But everywhere
      In his brain – day, night,
      As if on the air
      It were drawn rose-bright –
      Yea, far from that shore
Does he carry this vision of heretofore:

### IV

A ghost-girl-rider. And though, toil-tried,
      He withers daily,
      Time touches her not,
      But she still rides gaily
      In his rapt thought
      On that shagged and shaly
      Atlantic spot,
      And as when first eyed
Draws rein and sings to the swing of the tide.

*1913*


## THE SPELL OF THE ROSE

'I mean to build a hall anon,
      And shape two turrets there,
      And a broad newelled stair,
And a cool well for crystal water;
      Yes; I will build a hall anon,
      Plant roses love shall feed upon,
      And apple-trees and pear.'

He set to build the manor-hall,
      And shaped the turrets there,
      And the broad newelled stair,

And the cool well for crystal water;
   He built for me that manor-hall,
   And planted many trees withal,
     But no rose anywhere.

   And as he planted never a rose
     That bears the flower of love,
     Though other flowers throve
Some heart-bane moved our souls to sever
   Since he had planted never a rose;
   And misconceits raised horrid shows,
     And agonies came thereof.

   'I'll mend these miseries,' then said I,
     And so, at dead of night,
     I went and, screened from sight,
That nought should keep our souls in severance,
   I set a rose-bush. 'This', said I,
   'May end divisions dire and wry,
     And long-drawn days of blight.'

   But I was called from earth – yea, called
     Before my rose-bush grew;
     And would that now I knew
What feels he of the tree I planted,
   And whether, after I was called
   To be a ghost, he, as of old,
     Gave me his heart anew!

   Perhaps now blooms that queen of trees
     I set but saw not grow,
     And he, beside its glow –
Eyes couched of the mis-vision that blurred me –
   Ay, there beside that queen of trees
   He sees me as I was, though sees
     Too late to tell me so!

## ST LAUNCE'S REVISITED

Slip back, Time!
Yet again I am nearing
Castle and keep, uprearing
  Gray, as in my prime.

At the inn
Smiling nigh, why is it
Not as on my visit
  When hope and I were twin?

Groom and jade
Whom I found here, moulder;
Strange the tavern-holder,
  Strange the tap-maid.

Here I hired
Horse and man for bearing
Me on my wayfaring
  To the door desired.

Evening gloomed
As I journeyed forward
To the faces shoreward,
  Till their dwelling loomed.

If again
Towards the Atlantic sea there
I should speed, they'd be there
  Surely now as then? ...

Why waste thought,
When I know them vanished
Under earth; yea, banished
  Ever into nought!

# WHERE THE PICNIC WAS

Where we made the fire
In the summer time
Of branch and briar
On the hill to the sea,
I slowly climb
Through winter mire,
And scan and trace
The forsaken place
Quite readily.

Now a cold wind blows,
And the grass is gray,
But the spot still shows
As a burnt circle – aye,
And stick-ends, charred,
Still strew the sward
Whereon I stand,
Last relic of the band
Who came that day!

Yes, I am here
Just as last year,
And the sea breathes brine
From its strange straight line
Up hither, the same
As when we four came.
– But two have wandered far
From this grassy rise
Into urban roar
Where no picnics are,
And one – has shut her eyes
For evermore.

## HER SECRET

That love's dull smart distressed my heart
    He shrewdly learnt to see,
But that I was in love with a dead man
    Never suspected he.

He searched for the trace of a pictured face,
    He watched each missive come,
And a sheet that seemed like a love-line
    Wrought his look lurid and numb.

He dogged my feet to the city street,
    He followed me to the sea,
But not to the nigh, still churchyard
    Did he dream of following me!

## 'I ROSE UP AS MY CUSTOM IS'

I rose up as my custom is
    On the eve of All-Souls' day,
And left my grave for an hour or so
To call on those I used to know
    Before I passed away.

I visited my former Love
    As she lay by her husband's side;
I asked her if life pleased her, now
She was rid of a poet wrung in brow,
    And crazed with the ills he eyed;

Who used to drag her here and there
    Wherever his fancies led,
And point out pale phantasmal things,
And talk of vain vague purposings
    That she discredited.

She was quite civil, and replied,
  'Old comrade, is that you?
Well, on the whole, I like my life. –
I know I swore I'd be no wife,
  But what was I to do?

'You see, of all men for my sex
  A poet is the worst;
Women are practical, and they
Crave the wherewith to pay their way,
  And slake their social thirst.

'You were a poet – quite the ideal
  That we all love awhile:
But look at this man snoring here –
He's no romantic chanticleer,
  Yet keeps me in good style.

'He makes no quest into my thoughts,
  But a poet wants to know
What one has felt from earliest days,
Why one thought not in other ways,
  And one's Loves of long ago.'

Her words benumbed my fond faint ghost;
  The nightmares neighed from their stalls,
The vampires screeched, the harpies flew,
And under the dim dawn I withdrew
  To Death's inviolate halls.

# HAD YOU WEPT

Had you wept; had you but neared me with a hazed uncertain
    ray,
Dewy as the face of the dawn, in your large and luminous
    eye,
Then would have come back all the joys the tidings had slain
    that day,
And a new beginning, a fresh fair heaven, have smoothed the
    things awry.
But you were less feebly human, and no passionate need for
    clinging
Possessed your soul to overthrow reserve when I came near;
Ay, though you suffer as much as I from storms the hours
    are bringing
Upon your heart and mine, I never see you shed a tear.

The deep strong woman is weakest, the weak one is the
    strong;
The weapon of all weapons best for winning, you have not
    used;
Have you never been able, or would you not, through the
    evil times and long?
Has not the gift been given you, or such gift have you refused?
When I bade me not absolve you on that evening or the
    morrow,
Why did you not make war on me with those who weep like
    rain?
You felt too much, so gained no balm for all your torrid
    sorrow,
And hence our deep division, and our dark undying pain.

# IN THE BRITISH MUSEUM

'What do you see in that time-touched stone,
    When nothing is there
But ashen blankness, although you give it
    A rigid stare?

'You look not quite as if you saw,
    But as if you heard,
Parting your lips, and treading softly
    As mouse or bird.

'It is only the base of a pillar, they'll tell you,
    That came to us
From a far old hill men used to name
    Areopagus.'

– 'I know no art, and I only view
    A stone from a wall,
But I am thinking that stone has echoed
    The voice of Paul;

'Paul as he stood and preached beside it
    Facing the crowd,
A small gaunt figure with wasted features,
    Calling out loud

'Words that in all their intimate accents
    Pattered upon
That marble front, and were wide reflected,
    And then were gone.

'I'm a labouring man, and know but little,
    Or nothing at all;
But I can't help thinking that stone once echoed
    The voice of Paul.'

## SEEN BY THE WAITS

Through snowy woods and shady
  We went to play a tune
To the lonely manor-lady
  By the light of the Christmas moon.

We violed till, upward glancing
  To where a mirror leaned,
It showed her airily dancing,
  Deeming her movements screened;

Dancing alone in the room there,
  Thin-draped in her robe of night;
Her postures, glassed in the gloom there,
  Were a strange phantasmal sight.

She had learnt (we heard when homing)
  That her roving spouse was dead:
Why she had danced in the gloaming
  We thought, but never said.

## THE TWO SOLDIERS

Just at the corner of the wall
  We met – yes, he and I –
Who had not faced in camp or hall
  Since we bade home good-bye,
And what once happened came back – all –
  Out of those years gone by;

And that strange woman whom we knew
  And loved – long dead and gone,
Whose poor half-perished residue,
  Tombless and trod, lay yon,
But at this moment to our view
  Rose like a phantom wan!

And in his fixed face I could see,
  Lit by a lurid shine,
The drama re-enact which she
  Had dyed incarnadine
For us, and more. And doubtless he
  Beheld it too in mine.

A start, as at one slightly known;
  And with an indifferent air
We passed, without a sign being shown
  That, as it real were,
A memory-acted scene had thrown
  Its tragic shadow there.

# SATIRES OF CIRCUMSTANCE

## IN FIFTEEN GLIMPSES

### (First published April 1911)

### I

## AT TEA

The kettle descants in a cosy drone,
And the young wife looks in her husband's face,
And then at her guest's, and shows in her own
Her sense that she fills an envied place;
And the visiting lady is all abloom,
And says there was never so sweet a room.

And the happy young housewife does not know
That the woman beside her was first his choice,
Till the fates ordained it could not be so. . . .
Betraying nothing in look or voice
The guest sits smiling and sips her tea,
And he throws her a stray glance yearningly.

II

# IN CHURCH

'And now to God the Father', he ends,
And his voice thrills up to the topmost tiles:
Each listener chokes as he bows and bends,
And emotion pervades the crowded aisles.
Then the preacher glides to the vestry-door,
And shuts it, and thinks he is seen no more.

The door swings softly ajar meanwhile,
And a pupil of his in the Bible class,
Who adores him as one without gloss or guile,
Sees her idol stand with a satisfied smile
And re-enact at the vestry-glass
Each pulpit gesture in deft dumb-show
That had moved the congregation so.

III

# BY HER AUNT'S GRAVE

'Sixpence a week', says the girl to her lover,
'Aunt used to bring me, for she could confide
In me alone, she vowed. 'Twas to cover
The cost of her headstone when she died.
And that was a year ago last June;
I've not yet fixed it. But I must soon.'

'And where is the money now, my dear?'
'O, snug in my purse ... Aunt was *so* slow
In saving it – eighty weeks, or near.' ...
'Let's spend it', he hints. 'For she won't know.
There's a dance tonight at the Load of Hay.'
She passively nods. And they go that way.

## IV

# IN THE ROOM OF THE BRIDE-ELECT

'Would it had been the man of our wish!'
Sighs her mother. To whom with vehemence she
In the wedding-dress – the wife to be –
'Then why were you so mollyish
As not to insist on him for me!'
The mother, amazed: 'Why, dearest one,
Because you pleaded for this or none!'

'But Father and you should have stood out strong!
Since then, to my cost, I have lived to find
That you were right and that I was wrong;
This man is a dolt to the one declined. . . .
Ah! – here he comes with his button-hole rose.
Good God – I must marry him I suppose!'


## V

# AT A WATERING-PLACE

They sit and smoke on the esplanade,
The man and his friend, and regard the bay
Where the far chalk cliffs, to the left displayed,
Smile sallowly in the decline of day.
And saunterers pass with laugh and jest –
A handsome couple among the rest.

'That smart proud pair', says the man to his friend,
'Are to marry next week. . . . How little he thinks
That dozens of days and nights on end
I have stroked her neck, unhooked the links
Of her sleeve to get at her upper arm. . . .
Well, bliss is in ignorance: what's the harm!'

## VI

# IN THE CEMETERY

'You see those mothers squabbling there?'
Remarks the man of the cemetery.
'One says in tears, " 'Tis mine lies here!"
Another, "Nay, mine, you Pharisee!"
Another, "How dare you move my flowers
And put your own on this grave of ours!"
But all their children were laid therein
At different times, like sprats in a tin.

'And then the main drain had to cross,
And we moved the lot some nights ago,
And packed them away in the general foss
With hundreds more. But their folks don't know,
And as well cry over a new-laid drain
As anything else, to ease your pain!'

## VII

# OUTSIDE THE WINDOW

'My stick!' he says, and turns in the lane
To the house just left, whence a vixen voice
Comes out with the firelight through the pane,
And he sees within that the girl of his choice
Stands rating her mother with eyes aglare
For something said while he was there.

'At last I behold her soul undraped!'
Thinks the man who had loved her more than himself;
'My God! – 'tis but narrowly I have escaped. –
My precious porcelain proves it delf.'
His face has reddened like one ashamed,
And he steals off, leaving his stick unclaimed.

## VIII

# IN THE STUDY

He enters, and mute on the edge of a chair
Sits a thin-faced lady, a stranger there,
A type of decayed gentility;
And by some small signs he well can guess
That she comes to him almost breakfastless.

'I have called – I hope I do not err –
I am looking for a purchaser
Of some score volumes of the works
Of eminent divines I own, –
Left by my father – though it irks
My patience to offer them.' And she smiles
As if necessity were unknown;
'But the truth of it is that oftenwhiles
I have wished, as I am fond of art,
To make my rooms a little smart,
And these old books are so in the way.'
And lightly still she laughs to him,
As if to sell were a mere gay whim,
And that, to be frank, Life were indeed
To her not vinegar and gall,
But fresh and honey-like; and Need
No household skeleton at all.

## IX

# AT THE ALTAR-RAIL

'My bride is not coming, alas!' says the groom,
And the telegram shakes in his hand. 'I own
It was hurried! We met at a dancing-room
When I went to the Cattle-Show alone,
And then, next night, where the Fountain leaps,
And the Street of the Quarter-Circle sweeps.

'Ay, she won me to ask her to be my wife –
'Twas foolish perhaps! – to forsake the ways
Of the flaring town for a farmer's life.
She agreed. And we fixed it. Now she says:
"*It's sweet of you, dear, to prepare me a nest,*
*But a swift, short, gay life suits me best.*
*What I really am you have never gleaned;*
*I had eaten the apple ere you were weaned.*" '

## X

## IN THE NUPTIAL CHAMBER

'O that mastering tune!' And up in the bed
Like a lace-robed phantom springs the bride;
'And why?' asks the man she had that day wed,
With a start, as the band plays on outside.
'It's the townsfolk's cheery compliment
Because of our marriage, my Innocent.'

'O but you don't know! 'Tis the passionate air
To which my old Love waltzed with me,
And I swore as we spun that none should share
My home, my kisses, till death, save he!
And he dominates me and thrills me through,
And it's he I embrace while embracing you!'

## XI

## IN THE RESTAURANT

'But hear. If you stay, and the child be born,
It will pass as your husband's with the rest,
While, if we fly, the teeth of scorn
Will be gleaming at us from east to west;
And the child will come as a life despised;
I feel an elopement is ill-advised!'

'O you realize not what it is, my dear,
To a woman! Daily and hourly alarms
Lest the truth should out. How can I stay here
And nightly take him into my arms!
Come to the child no name or fame,
Let us go, and face it, and bear the shame.'


XII

## AT THE DRAPER'S

'I stood at the back of the shop, my dear,
  But you did not perceive me.
Well, when they deliver what you were shown
  I shall know nothing of it, believe me!'

And he coughed and coughed as she paled and said,
  'O, I didn't see you come in there –
Why couldn't you speak?' – 'Well, I didn't. I left
  That you should not notice I'd been there.

'You were viewing some lovely things. "*Soon required
  For a widow, of latest fashion*";
And I knew 'twould upset you to meet the man
  Who had to be cold and ashen

'And screwed in a box before they could dress you
  "*In the last new note in mourning*",
As they defined it. So, not to distress you,
  I left you to your adorning.'

## XIII

# ON THE DEATH-BED

'I'll tell – being past all praying for –
Then promptly die . . . He was out at the war,
And got some scent of the intimacy
That was under way between her and me;
And he stole back home, and appeared like a ghost
One night, at the very time almost
That I reached her house. Well I shot him dead,
And secretly buried him. Nothing was said.

'The news of the battle came next day;
He was scheduled missing. I hurried away,
Got out there, visited the field,
And sent home word that a search revealed
He was one of the slain; though, lying alone
And stript, his body had not been known.

'But she suspected. I lost her love,
Yea, my hope of earth, and of Heaven above;
And my time's now come, and I'll pay the score,
Though it be burning for evermore.'

## XIV

# OVER THE COFFIN

They stand confronting, the coffin between,
His wife of old, and his wife of late,
And the dead man whose they both had been
Seems listening aloof, as to things past date.
– 'I have called', says the first. 'Do you marvel or not?'
'In truth', says the second, 'I do – somewhat.'

127

'Well, there was a word to be said by me! . . .
I divorced that man because of you –
It seemed I must do it, boundenly;
But now I am older, and tell you true,
For life is little and dead lies he;
I would I had let alone you two!
And both of us, scorning parochial ways,
Had lived like the wives in the patriarchs' days.'

## XV

## IN THE MOONLIGHT

'O lonely workman, standing there
In a dream, why do you stare and stare
At her grave, as no other grave there were?

'If your great gaunt eyes so importune
Her soul by the shine of this corpse-cold moon,
Maybe you'll raise her phantom soon!'

'Why, fool, it is what I would rather see
Than all the living folk there be;
But alas, there is no such joy for me!'

'Ah – she was one you loved, no doubt,
Through good and evil, through rain and drought,
And when she passed, all your sun went out?'

'Nay: she was the woman I did not love,
Whom all the others were ranked above,
Whom during her life I thought nothing of.'

# AT THE WORD 'FAREWELL'

She looked like a bird from a cloud
    On the clammy lawn,
Moving alone, bare-browed
    In the dim of dawn.
The candles alight in the room
    For my parting meal
Made all things withoutdoors loom
    Strange, ghostly, unreal.

The hour itself was a ghost,
    And it seemed to me then
As of chances the chance furthermost
    I should see her again.
I beheld not where all was so fleet
    That a Plan of the past
Which had ruled us from birthtime to meet
    Was in working at last:

No prelude did I there perceive
    To a drama at all,
Or foreshadow what fortune might weave
    From beginnings so small;
But I rose as if quicked by a spur
    I was bound to obey,
And stepped through the casement to her
    Still alone in the gray.

'I am leaving you. . . . Farewell!' I said
    As I followed her on
By an alley bare boughs overspread;
    'I soon must be gone!'
Even then the scale might have been turned
    Against love by a feather,
– But crimson one cheek of hers burned
    When we came in together.

# FIRST SIGHT OF HER AND AFTER

A day is drawing to its fall
    I had not dreamed to see;
The first of many to enthrall
    My spirit, will it be?
Or is this eve the end of all
    Such new delight for me?

I journey home: the pattern grows
    Of moonshades on the way:
'Soon the first quarter, I suppose',
    Sky-glancing travellers say;
I realize that it, for those,
    Has been a common day.

# HEREDITY

I am the family face;
Flesh perishes, I live on,
Projecting trait and trace
Through time to times anon,
And leaping from place to place
Over oblivion.

The years-heired feature that can
In curve and voice and eye
Despise the human span
Of durance – that is I;
The eternal thing in man,
That heeds no call to die.

## ON A MIDSUMMER EVE

I idly cut a parsley stalk,
And blew therein towards the moon;
I had not thought what ghosts would walk
With shivering footsteps to my tune.

I went, and knelt, and scooped my hand
As if to drink, into the brook,
And a faint figure seemed to stand
Above me, with the bygone look.

I lipped rough rhymes of chance, not choice,
I thought not what my words might be;
There came into my ear a voice
That turned a tenderer verse for me.

## TIMING HER

*(Written to an old folk-tune)*

Lalage's coming:
Where is she now, O?
Turning to bow, O,
And smile, is she,
Just at parting,
Parting, parting,
As she is starting
To come to me?

Where is she now, O,
Now, and now, O,
Shadowing a bough, O,
Of hedge or tree
As she is rushing,
Rushing, rushing,
Gossamers brushing
To come to me?

Lalage's coming;
Where is she now, O;
Climbing the brow, O,
Of hills I see?
Yes, she is nearing,
Nearing, nearing,
Weather unfearing
To come to me.

Near is she now, O,
Now, and now, O;
Milk the rich cow, O,
Forward the tea;
Shake the down bed for her,
Linen sheets spread for her,
Drape round the head for her
Coming to me.

Lalage's coming,
She's nearer now, O,
End anyhow, O,
Today's husbandry!
Would a gilt chair were mine,
Slippers of vair were mine,
Brushes for hair were mine
Of ivory!

What will she think, O,
She who's so comely,
Viewing how homely
A sort are we!
Nothing resplendent,
No prompt attendant,
Not one dependent
Pertaining to me!

Lalage's coming;
Where is she now, O?
Fain I'd avow, O,

Full honestly
Nought here's enough for her,
All is too rough for her,
Even my love for her
Poor in degree.

She's nearer now, O,
Still nearer now, O,
She 'tis, I vow, O,
Passing the lea.
Rush down to meet her there,
Call out and greet her there.
Never a sweeter there
Crossed to me!

Lalage's come; aye,
Come is she now, O! . . .
Does Heaven allow, O,
A meeting to be?
Yes, she is here now,
Here now, here now,
Nothing to fear now,
Here's Lalage!

## THE BLINDED BIRD

So zestfully canst thou sing?
And all this indignity,
With God's consent, on thee!
Blinded ere yet a-wing
By the red-hot needle thou,
I stand and wonder how
So zestfully thou canst sing!

Resenting not such wrong,
Thy grievous pain forgot,
Eternal dark thy lot,

Groping thy whole life long,
After that stab of fire;
Enjailed in pitiless wire;
Resenting not such wrong!

Who hath charity? This bird.
Who suffereth long and is kind,
Is not provoked, though blind
And alive ensepulchred?
Who hopeth, endureth all things?
Who thinketh no evil, but sings?
Who is divine? This bird.

## 'I TRAVEL AS A PHANTOM NOW'

I travel as a phantom now,
For people do not wish to see
In flesh and blood so bare a bough
    As Nature makes of me.

And thus I visit bodiless
Strange gloomy households often at odds,
And wonder if Man's consciousness
    Was a mistake of God's.

And next I meet you, and I pause,
And think that if mistake it were,
As some have said, O then it was
    One that I well can bear!

*1915*

## LINES

### TO A MOVEMENT IN MOZART'S E FLAT SYMPHONY

Show me again the time
When in the Junetide's prime

We flew by meads and mountains northerly! –
Yea, to such freshness, fairness, fullness, fineness, freeness,
    Love lures life on.

    Show me again the day
    When from the sandy bay
We looked together upon the pestered sea! –
Yea, to such surging, swaying, sighing, swelling, shrinking,
    Love lures life on.

    Show me again the hour
    When by the pinnacled tower
We eyed each other and feared futurity! –
Yea, to such bodings, broodings, beatings, blanchings,
      blessings,
    Love lures life on.

    Show me again just this:
    The moment of that kiss
Away from the prancing folk, by the strawberry-tree! –
Yea, to such rashness, ratheness, rareness, ripeness, richness,
    Love lures life on.

*Begun November 1898*


# 'IN THE SEVENTIES'

'Qui deridetur ab amico suo sicut ego.' – Job

In the seventies I was bearing in my breast,
    Penned tight,
Certain starry thoughts that threw a magic light
On the worktimes and the soundless hours of rest
In the seventies; aye, I bore them in my breast
    Penned tight.

In the seventies when my neighbours – even my friend –
    Saw me pass,
Heads were shaken, and I heard the words, 'Alas,
For his onward years and name unless he mend!'
In the seventies, when my neighbours and my friend
    Saw me pass.

In the seventies those who met me did not know
    Of the vision
That immuned me from the chillings of misprision
And the damps that choked my goings to and fro
In the seventies; yea, those nodders did not know
    Of the vision.

In the seventies nought could darken or destroy it,
    Locked in me,
Though as delicate as lamp-worm's lucency;
Neither mist nor murk could weaken or alloy it
In the seventies! – could not darken or destroy it,
    Locked in me.


## THE PEDIGREE

### I

I bent in the deep of night
  Over a pedigree the chronicler gave
  As mine; and as I bent there, half-unrobed,
The uncurtained panes of my window-square let in the
    watery light
    Of the moon in its old age:
And green-rheumed clouds were hurrying past where mute
    and cold it globed
  Like a drifting dolphin's eye seen through a lapping wave.

II

So, scanning my sire-sown tree,
And the hieroglyphs of this spouse tied to that,
    With the offspring mapped below in lineage,
        Till the tangles troubled me,
The branches seemed to twist into a seared and cynic face
    Which winked and tokened towards the window like a
        Mage
    Enchanting me to gaze again thereat.

III

It was a mirror now,
    And in it a long perspective I could trace
Of my begetters, dwindling backward each past each
        All with the kindred look,
    Whose names had since been inked down in their place
        On the recorder's book,
Generation and generation of my mien, and build, and brow.

IV

And then did I divine
    That every heave and coil and move I made
Within my brain, and in my mood and speech,
        Was in the glass portrayed
    As long forestalled by their so making it;
The first of them, the primest fuglemen of my line,
Being fogged in far antiqueness past surmise and reason's
        reach.

V

Said I then, sunk in tone,
'I am merest mimicker and counterfeit! –
    Though thinking, *I am I,*
    *And what I do I do myself alone.*'
– The cynic twist of the page thereat unknit
Back to its normal figure, having wrought its purport wry,
    The Mage's mirror left the window-square,
    And the stained moon and drift retook their places there.

*1916*

# HIS HEART

## A WOMAN'S DREAM

At midnight, in the room where he lay dead
  Whom in his life I had never clearly read,
I thought if I could peer into that citadel
  His heart, I should at last know full and well

What hereto had been known to him alone,
  Despite our long sit-out of years foreflown,
'And if', I said, 'I do this for his memory's sake,
  It would not wound him, even if he could wake.'

So I bent over him. He seemed to smile
  With a calm confidence the whole long while
That I, withdrawing his heart, held it and, bit by bit,
  Perused the unguessed things found written on it.

It was inscribed like a terrestrial sphere
  With quaint vermiculations close and clear –
His graving. Had I known, would I have risked the stroke
  Its reading brought, and my own heart nigh broke!

Yes, there at last, eyes opened, did I see
  His whole sincere symmetric history;
There were his truth, his simple singlemindedness,
  Strained, maybe, by time's storms, but there no less.

There were the daily deeds from sun to sun
  In blindness, but good faith, that he had done;
There were regrets, at instances wherein he swerved
  (As he conceived) from cherishings I had deserved.

There were old hours all figured down as bliss –
  Those spent with me – (how little had I thought this!)
There those when, at my absence, whether he slept or waked,
  (Though I knew not 'twas so!) his spirit ached.

There that when we were severed, how day dulled
Till time joined us anew, was chronicled:
And arguments and battlings in defence of me
That heart recorded clearly and ruddily.

I put it back, and left him as he lay
While pierced the morning pink and then the gray
Into each dreary room and corridor around,
Where I shall wait, but his step will not sound.

## LIFE LAUGHS ONWARD

Rambling I looked for an old abode
Where, years back, one had lived I knew:
Its site a dwelling duly showed,
But it was new.

I went where, not so long ago,
The sod had riven two breasts asunder;
Daisies throve gaily there, as though
No grave were under.

I walked along a terrace where
Loud children gambolled in the sun:
The figure that had once sat there
Was missed by none.

Life laughed and moved on unsubdued,
I saw that Old succumbed to Young:
'Twas well. My too regretful mood
Died on my tongue.

## A MERRYMAKING IN QUESTION

'I will get a new string for my fiddle,
And call to the neighbours to come,
And partners shall dance down the middle
Until the old pewter-wares hum:
And we'll sip the mead, cyder, and rum!'

141

From the night came the oddest of answers:
  A hollow wind, like a bassoon,
And headstones all ranged up as dancers,
  And cypresses droning a croon,
  And gurgoyles that mouthed to the tune.


# A JANUARY NIGHT

## (1879)

  The rain smites more and more,
  The east wind snarls and sneezes;
Through the joints of the quivering door
  The water wheezes.

  The tip of each ivy-shoot
  Writhes on its neighbour's face;
There is some hid dread afoot
  That we cannot trace.

  Is it the spirit astray
  Of the man at the house below
Whose coffin they took in today?
  We do not know.


# THE OXEN

Christmas Eve, and twelve of the clock.
  'Now they are all on their knees',
An elder said as we sat in a flock
  By the embers in hearthside ease.

We pictured the meek mild creatures where
  They dwelt in their strawy pen,
Nor did it occur to one of us there
  To doubt they were kneeling then.

So fair a fancy few would weave
　　In these years! Yet, I feel,
If someone said on Christmas Eve,
　　'Come; see the oxen kneel

'In the lonely barton by yonder coomb
　　Our childhood used to know',
I should go with him in the gloom,
　　Hoping it might be so.

　　*1915*

# TRANSFORMATIONS

Portion of this yew
Is a man my grandsire knew,
Bosomed here at its foot:
This branch may be his wife,
A ruddy human life
Now turned to a green shoot.

These grasses must be made
Of her who often prayed,
Last century, for repose;
And the fair girl long ago
Whom I often tried to know
May be entering this rose.

So, they are not underground,
But as nerves and veins abound
In the growths of upper air,
And they feel the sun and rain,
And the energy again
That made them what they were!

# GREAT THINGS

Sweet cyder is a great thing,
  A great thing to me,
Spinning down to Weymouth town
  By Ridgway thirstily,
And maid and mistress summoning
  Who tend the hostelry:
O cyder is a great thing,
  A great thing to me!

The dance it is a great thing,
  A great thing to me,
With candles lit and partners fit
  For night-long revelry;
And going home when day-dawning
  Peeps pale upon the lea:
O dancing is a great thing,
  A great thing to me!

Love is, yea, a great thing,
  A great thing to me,
When, having drawn across the lawn
  In darkness silently,
A figure flits like one a-wing
  Out from the nearest tree:
O love is, yes, a great thing,
  A great thing to me!

Will these be always great things,
  Great things to me? . . .
Let it befall that One will call,
  'Soul, I have need of thee':
What then? Joy-jaunts, impassioned flings
  Love, and its ecstasy,
Will always have been great things,
  Great things to me!

# THE BLOW

That no man schemed it is my hope
Yea, that it fell by will and scope
    Of That Which some enthrone,
And for whose meaning myriads grope.

For I would not that of my kind
There should, of his unbiased mind,
    Have been one known
Who such a stroke could have designed,

Since it would augur works and ways
Below the lowest that man assays
    To have hurled that stone
Into the sunshine of our days!

And if it prove that no man did,
And that the Inscrutable, the Hid,
    Was cause alone
Of this foul crash our lives amid,

I'll go in due time, and forget
In some deep graveyard's oubliette
    The thing whereof I groan,
And cease from troubling; thankful yet

Time's finger should have stretched to show
No aimful author's was the blow
    That swept us prone,
But the Immanent Doer's That doth not know,

Which in some age unguessed of us
May lift Its blinding incubus,
    And see, and own:
'It grieves me I did thus and thus!'

## ON STURMINSTER FOOT-BRIDGE

### (Onomatopoeic)

Reticulations creep upon the slack stream's face
    When the wind skims irritably past,
The current clucks smartly into each hollow place
That years of flood have scrabbled in the pier's sodden base;
    The floating-lily leaves rot fast.

On a roof stand the swallows ranged in wistful waiting rows,
    Till they arrow off and drop like stones
Among the eyot-withies at whose foot the river flows:
And beneath the roof is she who in the dark world shows
    As a lattice-gleam when midnight moans.


## OLD FURNITURE

I know not how it may be with others
    Who sit amid relics of householdry
That date from the days of their mothers' mothers,
    But well I know how it is with me
      Continually.

I see the hands of the generations
    That owned each shiny familiar thing
In play on its knobs and indentations,
    And with its ancient fashioning
      Still dallying:

Hands behind hands, growing paler and paler,
    As in a mirror a candle-flame
Shows images of itself, each frailer
    As it recedes, though the eye may frame
      Its shape the same.

On the clock's dull dial a foggy finger,
    Moving to set the minutes right
With tentative touches that lift and linger
    In the wont of a moth on a summer night,
       Creeps to my sight.

On this old viol, too, fingers are dancing –
    As whilom – just over the strings by the nut,
The tip of a bow receding, advancing
    In airy quivers, as if it would cut
      The plaintive gut.

And I see a face by that box for tinder,
    Glowing forth in fits from the dark,
And fading again, as the linten cinder
    Kindles to red at the flinty spark,
      Or goes out stark.

Well, well. It is best to be up and doing,
    The world has no use for one today
Who eyes things thus – no aim pursuing!
    He should not continue in this stay,
      But sink away.

# THE INTERLOPER

'And I saw the figure and visage of Madness seeking for a home.'

There are three folk driving in a quaint old chaise,
    And the cliff-side track looks green and fair;
I view them talking in quiet glee
As they drop down towards the puffins' lair
    By the roughest of ways;
But another with the three rides on, I see,
    Whom I like not to be there!

No: it's not anybody you think of. Next
A dwelling appears by a slow sweet stream
Where two sit happy and half in the dark:
They read, helped out by a frail-wick'd gleam,
    Some rhythmic text;
But one sits with them whom they don't mark,
    One I'm wishing could not be there.

No: not whom you knew and name. And now
I discern gay diners in a mansion-place,
And the guests dropping wit – pert, prim, or choice,
And the hostess's tender and laughing face,
    And the host's bland brow;
But I cannot help hearing a hollow voice.
    And I'd fain not hear it there.

No: it's not from the stranger you met once. Ah,
Yet a goodlier scene than that succeeds;
People on a lawn – quite a crowd of them. Yes,
And they chatter and ramble as fancy leads;
    And they say, 'Hurrah!'
To a blithe speech made; save one, mirthless,
    Who ought not to be there.

Nay: it's not the pale Form your imagings raise,
That waits on us all at a destined time,
It is not the Fourth Figure the Furnace showed;
O that it were such a shape sublime
    In these latter days!
It is that under which best lives corrode;
    Would, would it could not be there!

# LOGS ON THE HEARTH

## A MEMORY OF A SISTER

The fire advances along the log
    Of the tree we felled,
Which bloomed and bore striped apples by the peck
    Till its last hour of bearing knelled.

The fork that first my hand would reach
    And then my foot
In climbings upward inch by inch, lies now
    Sawn, sapless, darkening with soot.

Where the bark chars is where, one year,
    It was pruned, and bled –
Then overgrew the wound. But now, at last,
    Its growings all have stagnated.

My fellow-climber rises dim
    From her chilly grave –
Just as she was, her foot near mine on the bending limb,
    Laughing, her young brown hand awave.

*December 1915*

# THE FIVE STUDENTS

The sparrow dips in his wheel-rut bath,
    The sun grows passionate-eyed,
And boils the dew to smoke by the paddock-path;
    As strenuously we stride, –
Five of us; dark He, fair He, dark She, fair She, I,
    All beating by.

The air is shaken, the high-road hot,
  Shadowless swoons the day,
The greens are sobered and cattle at rest; but not
  We on our urgent way, –
Four of us; fair She, dark She, fair He, I, are there,
  But one – elsewhere.

Autumn moulds the hard fruit mellow,
  And forward still we press
Through moors, briar-meshed plantations, clay-pits yellow,
  As in the spring hours – yes,
Three of us; fair He, fair She, I, as heretofore,
  But – fallen one more.

The leaf drops: earthworms draw it in
  At night-time noiselessly,
The fingers of birch and beech are skeleton-thin
  And yet on the beat are we, –
Two of us; fair She, I. But no more left to go
  The track we know.

Icicles tag the church-aisle leads,
  The flag-rope gibbers hoarse,
The home-bound foot-folk wrap their snow-flaked heads,
  Yet I still stalk the course –
One of us. . . . Dark and fair He, dark and fair She, gone:
  The rest – anon.


## DURING WIND AND RAIN

  They sing their dearest songs –
    He, she, all of them – yea,
  Treble and tenor and bass,
    And one to play;
  With the candles mooning each face. . . .
    Ah, no; the years O!
How the sick leaves reel down in throngs!

They clear the creeping moss –
Elders and juniors – aye,
Making the pathways neat
    And the garden gay;
And they build a shady seat. . . .
    Ah, no; the years, the years;
See, the white storm-birds wing across!

They are blithely breakfasting all –
Men and maidens – yea,
Under the summer tree,
    With a glimpse of the bay,
While pet fowl come to the knee. . . .
    Ah, no; the years O!
And the rotten rose is ript from the wall.

They change to a high new house,
He, she, all of them – aye,
Clocks and carpets and chairs
    On the lawn all day,
And brightest things that are theirs. . . .
    Ah, no; the years, the years;
Down their carved names the rain-drop ploughs.


# 'WHO'S IN THE NEXT ROOM?'

'Who's in the next room? – who?
    I seemed to see
Somebody in the dawning passing through,
    Unknown to me.'
'Nay: you saw nought. He passed invisibly.'

'Who's in the next room? – who?
    I seem to hear
Somebody muttering firm in a language new
    That chills the ear.'
'No: you catch not his tongue who has entered there.

'Who's in the next room? – who?
    I seem to feel
His breath like a clammy draught, as if it drew
    From the Polar Wheel.'
'No: none who breathes at all does the door conceal.'

'Who's in the next room? – who?
    A figure wan
With a message to one in there of something due?
    Shall I know him anon?'
'Yea he; and he brought such; and you'll know him anon.'

## THE MAN WITH A PAST

    There was merry-making
    When the first dart fell
    As a heralding, –
Till grinned the fully bared thing,
    And froze like a spell –
      Like a spell.

    Innocent was she,
    Innocent was I,
    Too simple we!
Before us we did not see,
    Nearing, aught wry –
      Aught wry!

    I can tell it not now,
    It was long ago;
    And such things cow;
But that is why and how
    Two lives were so –
      Were so.

    Yes, the years matured,
    And the blows were three
    That time ensured

On her, which she dumbly endured;
And one on me –
One on me.

# HE REVISITS HIS FIRST SCHOOL

I should not have shown in the flesh,
I ought to have gone as a ghost;
It was awkward, unseemly almost,
Standing solidly there as when fresh,
Pink, tiny, crisp-curled,
My pinions yet furled
From the winds of the world.

After waiting so many a year
To wait longer, and go as a sprite
From the tomb at the mid of some night
Was the right, radiant way to appear;
Not as one wanzing weak
From life's roar and reek,
His rest still to seek:

Yea, beglimpsed through the quaint quarried glass
Of green moonlight, by me greener made,
When they'd cry, perhaps, 'There sits his shade
In his olden haunt – just as he was
When in Walkingame he
Conned the grand Rule-of-Three
With the bent of a bee.'

But to show in the afternoon sun,
With an aspect of hollow-eyed care,
When none wished to see me come there.
Was a garish thing, better undone.
Yes; wrong was the way;
But yet, let me say,
I may right it – some day.

# FRAGMENT

At last I entered a long dark gallery,
　　Catacomb-lined; and ranged at the side
　　Were the bodies of men from far and wide
Who, motion past, were nevertheless not dead.

　'The sense of waiting here strikes strong;
Everyone's waiting, waiting, it seems to me;
　　What are you waiting for so long?
　　　What is to happen?' I said.

'O we are waiting for one called God,' said they,
　'(Though by some the Will, or Force, or Laws;
　　And, vaguely, by some, the Ultimate Cause;)
Waiting for him to see us before we are clay.
　　Yes; waiting, waiting, for God *to know it*.' . . .

　　'To know what?' questioned I.
'To know how things have been going on earth and below it:
　　It is clear he must know some day.'
　　I thereon asked them why.

'Since he made us humble pioneers
Of himself in consciousness of Life's tears,
It needs no mighty prophecy
To tell that what he could mindlessly show
His creatures, he himself will know.

'By some still close-cowled mystery
We have reached feeling faster than he,
But he will overtake us anon,
　　If the world goes on.'

## OLD EXCURSIONS

'What's the good of going to Ridgeway,
      Cerne, or Sydling Mill,
      Or to Yell'ham Hill,
Blithely bearing Casterbridge-way
      As we used to do?
She will no more climb up there,
Or be visible anywhere
      In those haunts we knew.'

But tonight, while walking weary,
      Near me seemed her shade,
      Come as 'twere to upbraid
This my mood in deeming dreary
      Scenes that used to please;
And, if she did come to me,
Still solicitous, there may be
      Good in going to these.

So, I'll care to roam to Ridgeway,
      Cerne, or Sydling Mill,
      Or to Yell'ham Hill,
Blithely bearing Casterbridge-way
      As we used to do.
Since her phasm may flit out there,
And may greet me anywhere
      In those haunts we knew.

   *April 1913*


## AN UPBRAIDING

Now I am dead you sing to me
      The songs we used to know,
But while I lived you had no wish
      Or care for doing so.

Now I am dead you come to me
    In the moonlight, comfortless;
Ah, what would I have given alive
    To win such tenderness!

When you are dead, and stand to me
    Not differenced, as now,
But like again, will you be cold
    As when we lived, or how?

## THE CHOIRMASTER'S BURIAL

He often would ask us
That, when he died,
After playing so many
To their last rest,
If out of us any
Should here abide,
And it would not task us,
We would with our lutes
Play over him
By his grave-brim
The psalm he liked best –
The one whose sense suits
'Mount Ephraim' –
And perhaps we should seem
To him, in Death's dream,
Like the seraphim.

As soon as I knew
That his spirit was gone
I thought this his due,
And spoke thereupon.
'I think', said the vicar,
'A read service quicker
Than viols out-of-doors
In these frosts and hoars.

That old-fashioned way
Requires a fine day,
And it seems to me
It had better not be.'

Hence, that afternoon,
Though never knew he
That his wish could not be,
To get through it faster
They buried the master
Without any tune.

But 'twas said that, when
At the dead of next night
The vicar looked out,
There struck on his ken
Thronged roundabout,
Where the frost was graying
The headstoned grass,
A band all in white
Like the saints in church-glass,
Singing and playing
The ancient stave
By the choirmaster's grave.

Such the tenor man told
When he had grown old.

# 'MEN WHO MARCH AWAY'

## (SONG OF THE SOLDIERS)

What of the faith and fire within us
    Men who march away
    Ere the barn-cocks say
    Night is growing gray,
Leaving all that here can win us;
What of the faith and fire within us
    Men who march away?

Is it a purblind prank, O think you,
  Friend with the musing eye,
  Who watch us stepping by
  With doubt and dolorous sigh?
Can much pondering so hoodwink you!
Is it a purblind prank, O think you,
  Friend with the musing eye?

Nay. We well see what we are doing,
  Though some may not see –
  Dalliers as they be –
  England's need are we;
Her distress would leave us rueing:
Nay. We well see what we are doing,
  Though some may not see!

In our heart of hearts believing
  Victory crowns the just,
  And that braggarts must
  Surely bite the dust,
Press we to the field ungrieving,
In our heart of hearts believing
  Victory crowns the just.

Hence the faith and fire within us
  Men who march away
  Ere the barn-cocks say
  Night is growing gray,
Leaving all that here can win us;
Hence the faith and fire within us
  Men who march away.

  *5 September 1914*

# IN TIME OF 'THE BREAKING OF NATIONS'[1]

### I

Only a man harrowing clods
   In a slow silent walk
With an old horse that stumbles and nods
   Half asleep as they stalk.

### II

Only thin smoke without flame
   From the heaps of couch-grass;
Yet this will go onward the same
   Though Dynasties pass.

### III

Yonder a maid and her wight
   Come whispering by:
War's annals will cloud into night
   Ere their story die.

*1915*

1. Jer. li: 20

# AFTERWARDS

When the Present has latched its postern behind my tremu-
   lous stay,
  And the May month flaps its glad green leaves like wings,
Delicate-filmed as new-spun silk, will the neighbours say,
  'He was a man who used to notice such things'?

If it be in the dusk when, like an eyelid's soundless blink,
  The dewfall-hawk comes crossing the shades to alight
Upon the wind-warped upland thorn, a gazer may think,
  'To him this must have been a familiar sight.'

If I pass during some nocturnal blackness, mothy and warm,
   When the hedgehog travels furtively over the lawn,
One may say, 'He strove that such innocent creatures should
     come to no harm,
    But he could do little for them; and now he is gone.'

If, when hearing that I have been stilled at last, they stand
   at the door,
    Watching the full-starred heavens that winter sees,
Will this thought rise on those who will meet my face no
   more,
    'He was one who had an eye for such mysteries'?

And will any say when my bell of quittance is heard in the
   gloom,
    And a crossing breeze cuts a pause in its outrollings,
Till they rise again, as they were a new bell's boom,
    'He hears it not now, but used to notice such things'?

# 6

*from*

## LATE LYRICS AND EARLIER

# WEATHERS

### I

This is the weather the cuckoo likes,
    And so do I;
When showers betumble the chestnut spikes,
    And nestlings fly:
And the little brown nightingale bills his best,
And they sit outside at 'The Travellers' Rest',
And maids come forth sprig-muslin drest,
And citizens dream of the south and west,
    And so do I.

### II

This is the weather the shepherd shuns,
    And so do I;
When beeches drip in browns and duns,
    And thresh, and ply;
And hill-hid tides throb, throe on throe,
And meadow rivulets overflow,
And drops on gate-bars hang in a row,
And rooks in families homeward go,
    And so do I.


# SUMMER SCHEMES

When friendly summer calls again,
    Calls again
Her little fifers to these hills,
We'll go – we two – to that arched fane
Of leafage where they prime their bills
Before they start to flood the plain
With quavers, minims, shakes, and trills.
    ' – We'll go', I sing; but who shall say
    What may not chance before that day!

And we shall see the waters spring,
    Waters spring
From chinks the scrubby copses crown;
And we shall trace their oncreeping
To where the cascade tumbles down
And sends the bobbing growths aswing,
And ferns not quite but almost drown.
    ' – We shall', I say; but who may sing
    Of what another moon will bring!


## 'I SOMETIMES THINK'

### (FOR F. E. H.)

I sometimes think as here I sit
    Of things I have done,
Which seemed in doing not unfit
    To face the sun:
Yet never a soul has paused a whit
    On such – not one.

There was that eager strenuous press
    To sow good seed;
There was that saving from distress
    In the nick of need;
There were those words in the wilderness:
    Who cared to heed?

Yet can this be full true, or no?
    For one did care,
And, spiriting into my house, to, fro,
    Like wind on the stair,
Cares still, heeds all, and will, even though
    I may despair.

# THE STRANGE HOUSE

## (MAX GATE, A.D. 2000)

'I hear the piano playing –
  Just as a ghost might play.'
' – O, but what are you saying?
  There's no piano today;
Their old one was sold and broken:
  Years past it went amiss.'
' – I heard it, or shouldn't have spoken:
    A strange house, this!

'I catch some undertone here,
  From some one out of sight.'
' – Impossible; we are alone here,
  And shall be through the night.'
' – The parlour-door – what stirred it?'
  ' – No one: no soul's in range.'
' – But, anyhow, I heard it,
    And it seems strange!

'Seek my own room I cannot –
  A figure is on the stair!'
' – What figure? Nay, I scan not
  Any one lingering there.
A bough outside is waving,
  And that's its shade by the moon.'
' – Well, all is strange! I am craving
    Strength to leave soon.'

' – Ah, maybe you've some vision
  Of showings beyond our sphere;
Some sight, sense, intuition
  Of what once happened here?
The house is old; they've hinted
  It once held two love-thralls,
And they may have imprinted
    Their dreams on its walls?

'They were – I think 'twas told me –
    Queer in their works and ways;
The teller would often hold me
    With weird tales of those days.
Some folk can not abide here,
    But we – we do not care
Who loved, laughed, wept, or died here,
      Knew joy, or despair.'


# THE WOMAN I MET


A stranger, I threaded sunken-hearted
    A lamp-lit crowd;
And anon there passed me a soul departed,
    Who mutely bowed.
In my far-off youthful years I had met her,
Full-pulsed; but now, no more life's debtor,
    Onward she slid
  In a shroud that furs half-hid.

'Why do you trouble me, dead woman,
    Trouble me;
You whom I knew when warm and human?
    – How it be
That you quitted earth and are yet upon it
Is, to any who ponder on it,
    Past being read!'
  'Still, it is so', she said.

'These were my haunts in my olden sprightly
    Hours of breath;
Here I went tempting frail youth nightly
    To their death;
But you deemed me chaste – me, a tinselled sinner!
How thought you one with pureness in her
    Could pace this street
  Eyeing some man to greet?

'Well; your very simplicity made me love you
        Mid such town dross,
Till I set not Heaven itself above you,
        Who grew my Cross;
For you'd only nod, despite how I sighed for you;
So you tortured me, who fain would have died for you!
        – What I suffered then
        Would have paid for the sins of ten!


'Thus went the days. I feared you despised me
        To fling me a nod
Each time, no more: till love chastised me
        As with a rod
That a fresh bland boy of no assurance
Should fire me with passion beyond endurance,
        While others all
        I hated, and loathed their call.


'I said: "It is his mother's spirit
        Hovering around
To shield him, maybe!" I used to fear it,
        As still I found
My beauty left no least impression,
And remnants of pride withheld confession
        Of my true trade
        By speaking; so I delayed.


'I said: "Perhaps with a costly flower
        He'll be beguiled."
I held it, in passing you one late hour,
        To your face: you smiled,
Keeping step with the throng; though you did not see
    there
A single one that rivalled me there! . . .
        Well: it's all past.
        I died in the Lock at last.'

So walked the dead and I together
    The quick among,
Elbowing our kind of every feather
    Slowly and long;
Yea, long and slowly. That a phantom should stalk there
With me seemed nothing strange, and talk there
    That winter night
    By flaming jets of light.

She showed me Juans who feared their call-time,
    Guessing their lot;
She showed me her sort that cursed their fall-time,
    And that did not.
Till suddenly murmured she: 'Now, tell me,
Why asked you never, ere death befell me,
    To have my love,
    Much as I dreamt thereof?'

I could not answer. And she, well weeting
    All in my heart,
Said: 'God your guardian kept our fleeting
    Forms apart!'
Sighing and drawing her furs around her
Over the shroud that tightly bound her,
    With wafts as from clay
    She turned and thinned away.

*London, 1918*

# THE FALLOW DEER AT THE LONELY
# HOUSE

One without looks in tonight
    Through the curtain-chink
From the sheet of glistening white;
One without looks in tonight
    As we sit and think
    By the fender-brink.

We do not discern those eyes
    Watching in the snow;
Lit by lamps of rosy dyes
We do not discern those eyes
    Wondering, aglow,
    Fourfooted, tiptoe.

## THE SELFSAME SONG

A bird sings the selfsame song,
With never a fault in its flow,
That we listened to here those long
    Long years ago.

A pleasing marvel is how
A strain of such rapturous rote
Should have gone on thus till now
    Unchanged in a note!

– But it's not the selfsame bird. –
No: perished to dust is he. . . .
As also are those who heard
    That song with me.

## AT LULWORTH COVE A CENTURY BACK

Had I but lived a hundred years ago
I might have gone, as I have gone this year,
By Warmwell Cross on to a Cove I know,
And Time have placed his finger on me there:

'*You see that man?* – I might have looked, and said,
'O yes: I see him. One that boat has brought
Which dropped down Channel round Saint Alban's Head.
So commonplace a youth calls not my thought.'

'*You see that man?*' – 'Why yes; I told you; yes:
Of an idling town-sort; thin; hair brown in hue;
And as the evening light scants less and less
He looks up at a star, as many do.'

'*You see that man?*' – 'Nay, leave me!' then I plead,
'I have fifteen miles to vamp across the lea,
And it grows dark, and I am weary-kneed:
I have said the third time; yes, that man I see!'

'Good. That man goes to Rome – to death, despair;
And no one notes him now but you and I:
A hundred years, and the world will follow him there,
And bend with reverence where his ashes lie.'

*September 1920*

NOTE. In September 1820 Keats, on his way to Rome, landed one day
on the Dorset coast, and composed the sonnet, 'Bright star! would I
were steadfast as thou art'. The spot of his landing is judged to have
been Lulworth Cove.

# A MAIDEN'S PLEDGE

## (SONG)

I do not wish to win your vow
To take me soon or late as bride,
And lift me from the nook where now
I tarry your farings to my side.
I am blissful ever to abide
In this green labyrinth – let all be,
If but, whatever may betide,
You do not leave off loving me!

Your comet-comings I will wait
With patience time shall not wear through;
The yellowing years will not abate
My largened love and truth to you,

Nor drive me to complaint undue
Of absence, much as I may pine,
If never another 'twixt us two
Shall come, and you stand wholly mine.


## THE BEAUTY

O do not praise my beauty more
   In such word-wild degree,
And say I am one all eyes adore;
   For these things harass me!

But do for ever softly say:
   'From now unto the end
Come weal, come wanzing, come what may,
   Dear, I will be your friend.'

I hate my beauty in the glass:
   My beauty is not I:
I wear it: none cares whether, alas,
   Its wearer live or die!

The inner I O care for, then,
   Yea, me and what I am,
And shall be at the gray hour when
   My cheek begins to clam.

NOTE. 'The Regent Street beauty, Miss Verrey, the Swiss confectioner's daughter, whose personal attractions have been so mischievously exaggerated, died of fever on Monday evening, brought on by the annoyance she had been for some time subject to.' – London paper, October 1828

## 'SHE DID NOT TURN'

> She did not turn,
> But passed foot-faint with averted head
> In her gown of green, by the bobbing fern,
> Though I leaned over the gate that led
> From where we waited with table spread;
>     But she did not turn:
> Why was she near there if love had fled?

> She did not turn,
> Though the gate was whence I had often sped
> In the mists of morning to meet her, and learn
> Her heart, when its moving moods I read
> As a book – she mine, as she sometimes said;
>     But she did not turn,
> And passed foot-faint with averted head.

## AFTER THE WAR

> Last Post sounded
> Across the mead
> To where he loitered
> With absent heed.
> Five years before
> In the evening there
> Had flown that call
> To him and his Dear.
> 'You'll never come back;
> Good-bye!' she had said;
> 'Here I'll be living,
> And my Love dead!'

> Those closing minims
> Had been as shafts darting
> Through him and her pressed
> In that last parting;

They thrilled him not now,
In the selfsame place
With the selfsame sun
On his war-seamed face.
'Lurks a god's laughter
In this?' he said,
'That I am the living
And she the dead!'


## 'IF YOU HAD KNOWN'

If you had known
When listening with her to the far-down moan
Of the white-selvaged and empurpled sea,
And rain came on that did not hinder talk,
Or damp your flashing facile gaiety
In turning home, despite the slow wet walk
By crooked ways, and over stiles of stone;
If you had known

You would lay roses,
Fifty years thence, on her monument, that discloses
Its graying shape upon the luxuriant green;
Fifty years thence to an hour, by chance led there,
What might have moved you? – yea, had you foreseen
That on the tomb of the selfsame one, gone where
The dawn of every day is as the close is,
You would lay roses!

*1920*


## THE CHAPEL-ORGANIST

### (A.D. 185–)

I've been thinking it through, as I play here tonight, to play
never again,
By the light of that lowering sun peering in at the window-
pane,

And over the back-street roofs, throwing shades from the
    boys of the chore
In the gallery, right upon me, sitting up to these keys once
    more. . . .
How I used to hear tongues ask, as I sat here when I was new:
'Who is she playing the organ? She touches it mightily true!'
'She travels from Havenpool Town', the deacon would softly
    speak,
'The stipend can hardly cover her fare hither twice in the
    week.'
(It fell far short of doing, indeed; but I never told,
For I have craved minstrelsy more than lovers, or beauty,
    or gold.)

'Twas so he answered at first, but the story grew different
    later:
'It cannot go on much longer, from what we hear of her
    now!'
At the meaning wheeze in the words the inquirer would
    shift his place
Till he could see round the curtain that screened me from
    people below.
'A handsome girl', he would murmur, upstaring (and so
    I am).
'But – too much sex in her build; fine eyes, but eyelids too
    heavy;
A bosom too full for her age; in her lips too voluptuous a
    dye.'
(It may be. But who put it there? Assuredly it was not I.)

I went on playing and singing when this I had heard, and
    more,
Though tears half-blinded me; yes, I remained going on and
    on,
Just as I used me to chord and to sing at the selfsame time! . . .
For it's a contralto – my voice is; they'll hear it again here
    tonight
In the psalmody notes that I love far beyond every lower
    delight.

Well, the deacon, in fact, that day had learnt new tidings
    about me;
They troubled his mind not a little, for he was a worthy man.
(He trades as a chemist in High Street, and during the week
    he had sought
His fellow-deacon, who throve as a bookbinder over the way.)
'These are strange rumours', he said. 'We must guard the
    good name of the chapel.
If, sooth, she's of evil report, what else can we do but dismiss
    her?'
' – But get such another to play here we cannot for double
    the price!'
It settled the point for the time, and I triumphed awhile in
    their strait,
And my much-beloved grand semibreves went living on,
    pending my fate.


At length in the congregation more headshakes and
    murmurs were rife,
And my dismissal was ruled, though I was not warned of it
    then.
But a day came when they declared it. The news entered
    me as a sword;
I was broken; so pallid of face that they thought I should
    faint, they said.
I rallied. 'O, rather than go, I will play you for nothing!'
    said I.
'Twas in much desperation I spoke it, for bring me to forfeit
    I could not
Those melodies chorded so richly for which I had laboured
    and lived.
They paused. And for nothing I played at the chapel through
    Sundays again,
Upheld by that art which I loved more than blandishments
    lavished of men.


But it fell that murmurs anew from the flock broke the
    pastor's peace.

Some member had seen me at Havenpool, comrading close
    a sea-captain.
(O yes; I was thereto constrained, lacking means for the fare
    to and fro.)
Yet God knows, if aught He knows ever, I loved the Old-
    Hundredth, Saint Stephen's,
Mount Zion, New Sabbath, Miles-Lane, Holy Rest, and
    Arabia, and Eaton,
Above all embraces of body by wooers who sought me and
    won! . . .
Next week 'twas declared I was seen coming home with a
    swain ere the sun.


The deacons insisted then, strong; and forgiveness I did not
    implore.
I saw all was lost for me, quite, but I made a last bid in my
    throbs.
My bent, finding victual in lust, men's senses had libelled
    my soul,
But the soul should die game, if I knew it! I turned to my
    masters and said:
'I yield, Gentlemen, without parlance. But – let me just
    hymn you *once* more!
It's a little thing, Sirs, that I ask; and a passion is music
    with me!'
They saw that consent would cost nothing, and show as
    good grace, as knew I,
Though tremble I did, and feel sick, as I paused thereat,
    dumb for their words.
They gloomily nodded assent, saying, 'Yes, if you care to.
    Once more,
And only once more, understand.' To that with a bend I
    agreed.
– 'You've a fixed and a far-reaching look', spoke one who
    had eyed me awhile.
'I've a fixed and a far-reaching plan, and my look only showed
    it', I smile.

This evening of Sunday is come – the last of my functioning
here.

'She plays as if she were possessed!' they exclaim, glancing
upward and round.

'Such harmonies I never dreamt the old instrument capable
of!'

Meantime the sun lowers and goes; shades deepen; the lights
are turned up,

And the people voice out the last singing: tune Tallis: the
Evening Hymn.

(I wonder Dissenters sing Ken: it shows them more liberal
in spirit

At this little chapel down here than at certain new others I
know.)

I sing as I play. Murmurs some one: 'No woman's throat
richer than hers!'

'True: in these parts,' think I. 'But, my man, never more
will its richness outspread.'

And I sing with them onward: 'The grave dread as little do I
as my bed.'


I lift up my feet from the pedals; and then, while my eyes
are still wet

From the symphonies born of my fingers, I do that whereon
I am set,

And draw from my 'full round bosom' (their words; how can
I help its heave?)

A bottle blue-coloured and fluted – a vinaigrette, they may
conceive –

And before the choir measures my meaning, reads aught in
my moves to and fro,

I drink from the phial at a draught, and they think it a
pick-me-up; so.

Then I gather my books as to leave, bend over the keys as
to pray.

When they come to me motionless, stooping, quick death
will have whisked me away.

'Sure, nobody meant her to poison herself in her haste, after
    all!'
The deacons will say as they carry me down and the night
    shadows fall,
'Though the charges were true,' they will add. 'It's a case red
    as scarlet withal!'
I have never once minced it. Lived chaste I have not. Heaven
    knows it above! . . .
But past all the heavings of passion – it's music has been my
    life-love! . . .
That tune did go well – this last playing! . . . I reckon they'll
    bury me here. . . .
Not a soul from the seaport my birthplace – will come, or
    bestow me . . . a tear.

## AFTER A ROMANTIC DAY

The railway bore him through
An earthen cutting out from a city:
    There was no scope for view,
Though the frail light shed by a slim young moon
    Fell like a friendly tune.

    Fell like a liquid ditty,
And the blank lack of any charm
    Of landscape did no harm.
The bald steep cutting, rigid, rough,
    And moon-lit, was enough
For poetry of place: its weathered face
Formed a convenient sheet whereon
The visions of his mind were drawn.

## IN THE SMALL HOURS

I lay in my bed and fiddled
  With a dreamland viol and bow,
And the tunes flew back to my fingers
  I had melodied years ago.
It was two or three in the morning
  When I fancy-fiddled so
Long reels and country-dances,
  And hornpipes swift and slow.

And soon anon came crossing
  The chamber in the gray
Figures of jigging fieldfolk –
  Saviours of corn and hay –
To the air of 'Haste to the Wedding',
  As after a wedding-day;
Yea, up and down the middle
  In windless whirls went they!

There danced the bride and bridegroom,
  And couples in a train,
Gay partners time and travail
  Had longwhiles stilled amain! . . .
It seemed a thing for weeping
  To find, at slumber's wane
And morning's sly increeping,
  That Now, not Then, held reign.

## LAST WORDS TO A DUMB FRIEND

Pet was never mourned as you,
Purrer of the spotless hue,
Plumy tail, and wistful gaze
While you humoured our queer ways,

Or outshrilled your morning call
Up the stairs and through the hall –
Foot suspended in its fall –
While, expectant, you would stand
Arched, to meet the stroking hand;
Till your way you chose to wend
Yonder, to your tragic end.

Never another pet for me!
Let your place all vacant be;
Better blankness day by day
Than companion torn away.
Better bid his memory fade,
Better blot each mark he made,
Selfishly escape distress
By contrived forgetfulness,
Than preserve his prints to make
Every morn and eve an ache.
From the chair whereon he sat
Sweep his fur, nor wince thereat:
Rake his little pathways out
Mid the bushes roundabout;
Smooth away his talons' mark
From the claw-worn pine-tree bark,
Where he climbed as dusk embrowned,
Waiting us who loitered round.

Strange it is this speechless thing,
Subject to our mastering,
Subject for his life and food
To our gift, and time, and mood.
Timid pensioner of us Powers,
His existence ruled by ours,
Should – by crossing at a breath
Into safe and shielded death,
By the merely taking hence
Of his insignificance –
Loom as largened to the sense,

Shape as part, above man's will,
Of the Imperturbable.

As a prisoner, flight debarred,
Exercising in a yard,
Still retain I, troubled, shaken,
Mean estate, by him forsaken;
And this home, which scarcely took
Impress from his little look,
By his faring to the Dim
Grows all eloquent of him.

Housemate, I can think you still
Bounding to the window-sill,
Over which I vaguely see
Your small mound beneath the tree,
Showing in the autumn shade
That you moulder where you played.

*2 October 1904*


# AN ANCIENT TO ANCIENTS

Where once we danced, where once we sang,
    Gentlemen,
The floors are sunken, cobwebs hang,
And cracks creep; worms have fed upon
The doors. Yea, sprightlier times were then
Than now, with harps and tabrets gone,
    Gentlemen!

Where once we rowed, where once we sailed,
    Gentlemen,
And damsels took the tiller, veiled
Against too strong a stare (God wot
Their fancy, then or anywhen!)
Upon that shore we are clean forgot,
    Gentlemen!

We have lost somewhat, afar and near,
      Gentlemen,
The thinning of our ranks each year
Affords a hint we are nigh undone,
That we shall not be ever again
The marked of many, loved of one,
      Gentlemen.

In dance the polka hit our wish,
      Gentlemen,
The paced quadrille, the spry schottische,
'Sir Roger'. – And in opera spheres
The 'Girl' (the famed 'Bohemian'),
And 'Trovatore', held the ears,
      Gentlemen.

This season's paintings do not please,
      Gentlemen,
Like Etty, Mulready, Maclise;
Throbbing romance has waned and wanned;
No wizard wields the witching pen
Of Bulwer, Scott, Dumas, and Sand,
      Gentlemen.

The bower we shrined to Tennyson,
      Gentlemen,
Is roof-wrecked; damps there drip upon
Sagged seats, the creeper-nails are rust,
The spider is sole denizen;
Even she who voiced those rhymes is dust,
      Gentlemen!

We who met sunrise sanguine-souled,
      Gentlemen,
Are wearing weary. We are old;
These younger press; we feel our rout
Is imminent to Aïdes' den –
That evening shades are stretching out,
      Gentlemen!

And yet, though ours be failing frames,
        Gentlemen,
So were some others' history names,
Who trode their track light-limbed and fast
As these youth, and not alien
From enterprise, to their long last,
        Gentlemen.

Sophocles, Plato, Socrates,
        Gentlemen,
Pythagoras, Thucydides,
Herodotus, and Homer – yea,
Clement, Augustin, Origen,
Burnt brightlier towards their setting-day,
        Gentlemen.

And ye, red-lipped and smooth-browed; list,
        Gentlemen;
Much is there waits you we have missed;
Much lore we leave you worth the knowing,
Much, much has lain outside our ken:
Nay, rush not: time serves: we are going,
        Gentlemen.

# SURVIEW

'Cogitavi vias meas'

A cry from the green-grained sticks of the fire
    Made me gaze where it seemed to be:
'Twas my own voice talking therefrom to me
On how I had walked when my sun was higher
    My heart in its arrogancy.

'*You held not to whatsoever was true*',
    Said my own voice talking to me:
'*Whatsoever was just you were slack to see;*
*Kept not things lovely and pure in view*',
    Said my own voice talking to me.

'*You slighted her that endureth all*',
 Said my own voice talking to me;
'*Vaunteth not, trusteth hopefully;*
*That suffereth long and is kind withal*',
 Said my own voice talking to me.

'*You taught not that which you set about*',
 Said my own voice talking to me;
'*That the greatest of things is Charity. . . .*'
– And the sticks burnt low, and the fire went out,
 And my voice ceased talking to me.

# 7

*from*

## HUMAN SHOWS, FAR PHANTASIES, SONGS, AND TRIFLES

# WAITING BOTH

A star looks down at me,
And says: 'Here I and you
Stand, each in our degree:
What do you mean to do, –
    Mean to do?'

I say: 'For all I know,
Wait, and let Time go by,
Till my change come.' – 'Just so,'
The star says: 'So mean I: –
    So mean I.'


# 'ANY LITTLE OLD SONG'

Any little old song
    Will do for me,
Tell it of joys gone long,
    Or joys to be,
Or friendly faces best
    Loved to see.

Newest themes I want not
    On subtle strings,
And for thrillings pant not
    That new song brings:
I only need the homeliest
    Of heartstirrings.


# AT RUSHY-POND

On the frigid face of the heath-hemmed pond
    There shaped the half-grown moon:
Winged whiffs from the north with a husky croon
    Blew over and beyond.

And the wind flapped the moon in its float on the pool,
    And stretched it to oval form;
Then corkscrewed it like a wriggling worm;
    Then wanned it weariful.

And I cared not for conning the sky above
    Where hung the substant thing,
For my thought was earthward sojourning
    On the scene I had vision of.

Since there it was once, in a secret year,
    I had called a woman to me
From across this water, ardently –
    And practised to keep her near;

Till the last weak love-words had been said,
    And ended was her time,
And blurred the bloomage of her prime,
    And white the earlier red.

And the troubled orb in the pond's sad shine
    Was her very wraith, as scanned
When she withdrew thence, mirrored, and
    Her days dropped out of mine.

# A SPELLBOUND PALACE

## (HAMPTON COURT)

On this kindly yellow day of mild low-travelling winter sun
    The stirless depths of the yews
    Are vague with misty blues:
Across the spacious pathways stretching spires of shadow run,
And the wind-gnawed walls of ancient brick are fired
    vermillion

Two or three early sanguine finches tune
Some tentative strains, to be enlarged by May or June:
From a thrush or blackbird
Comes now and then a word,
While an enfeebled fountain somewhere within is heard.

Our footsteps wait awhile,
Then draw beneath the pile,
When an inner court outspreads
As 'twere History's own asile,
Where the now-visioned fountain its attenuate crystal sheds
In passive lapse that seems to ignore the yon world's clamor-
ous clutch,
And lays an insistent numbness on the place, like a cold
hand's touch.

And there swaggers the Shade of a straddling King, plumed,
sworded, with sensual face,
And lo, too, that of his Minister, at a bold self-centred pace:
Sheer in the sun they pass; and thereupon all is still,
Save the mindless fountain tinkling on with thin enfeebled
will.

## WHEN DEAD

### TO —

It will be much better when
I am under the bough;
I shall be more myself, Dear, then,
Than I am now.

No sign of querulousness
To wear you out
Shall I show there: strivings and stress
Be quite without.

This fleeting life-brief blight
Will have gone past
When I resume my old and right
Place in the Vast.

And when you come to me
To show you true,
Doubt not I shall infallibly
Be waiting you.


# THE GRAVEYARD OF DEAD CREEDS

I lit upon the graveyard of dead creeds
In wistful wanderings through old wastes of thought,
Where bristled fennish fungi, fruiting nought,
Amid the sepulchres begirt with weeds,

Which stone by stone recorded sanct, deceased
Catholicons that had, in centuries flown,
Physicked created man through his long groan,
Ere they went under, all their potence ceased.

When in a breath-while, lo, their spectres rose
Like wakened winds that autumn summons up: –
'Out of us cometh an heir, that shall disclose
New promise!' cried they. 'And the caustic cup

'We ignorantly upheld to men, be filled
With draughts more pure than those we ever distilled,
That shall make tolerable to sentient seers
The melancholy marching of the years.'

## A SHEEP FAIR

The day arrives of the autumn fair,
    And torrents fall,
Though sheep in throngs are gathered there,
    Ten thousand all,
Sodden, with hurdles round them reared:
And, lot by lot, the pens are cleared,
And the auctioneer wrings out his beard,
And wipes his book, bedrenched and smeared,
And rakes the rain from his face with the edge of his hand,
    As torrents fall.

## SNOW IN THE SUBURBS

Every branch big with it,
Bent every twig with it;
Every fork like a white web-foot;
Every street and pavement mute:
Some flakes have lost their way, and grope back upward, when
Meeting those meandering down they turn and descend again.
The palings are glued together like a wall,
And there is no waft of wind with the fleecy fall.

A sparrow enters the tree,
Whereon immediately
A snow-lump thrice his own slight size
Descends on him and showers his head and eyes,
And overturns him,
And near inurns him,
And lights on a nether twig, when its brush
Starts off a volley of other lodging lumps with a rush.

The steps are a blanched slope,
Up which, with feeble hope,
A black cat comes, wide-eyed and thin;
And we take him in.


# THE FROZEN GREENHOUSE

## (ST JULIOT)

'There was a frost
Last night!' she said,
'And the stove was forgot
When we went to bed,
And the greenhouse plants
Are frozen dead!'

By the breakfast blaze
Blank-faced spoke she,
Her scared young look
Seeming to be
The very symbol
Of tragedy.

The frost is fiercer
Than then today,
As I pass the place
Of her once dismay,
But the greenhouse stands
Warm, tight, and gay,

While she who grieved
At the sad lot
Of her pretty plants –
Cold, iced, forgot –
Herself is colder,
And knows it not.

## AN EXPOSTULATION

Why want to go afar
    Where pitfalls are,
When all we swains adore
Your featness more and more
As heroine of our artless masquings here,
And count few Wessex' daughters half so dear?

Why paint your appealing face,
    When its born grace
Is such no skill can match
With powder, puff, or patch,
Whose every touch defames your bloomfulness,
And with each stain increases our distress?

Yea, is it not enough
    That (rare or rough
Your lines here) all uphold you,
And as with wings enfold you,
But you must needs desert the kine-cropt vale
Wherein your foredames gaily filled the pail?

## HE INADVERTENTLY CURES HIS LOVE-PAINS

### (SONG)

I said: 'O let me sing the praise
Of her who sweetly racks my days, –
    Her I adore;
Her lips, her eyes, her moods, her ways!'

In miseries of pulse and pang
I strung my harp, and straightway sang
    As none before: –
To wondrous words my quavers rang!

Thus I let heartaches lilt my verse,
Which suaged and soothed, and made disperse
    The smarts I bore
To stagnance like a sepulchre's.

But, eased, the days that thrilled ere then
Lost value; and I ask, O when,
    And how, restore
Those old sweet agonies again!

# INSCRIPTIONS FOR A PEAL OF EIGHT BELLS

## AFTER A RESTORATION

I. Thomas Tremble new-made me
Eighteen hundred and fifty-three:
Why he did I fail to see.

II. I was well-toned by William Brine,
Seventeen hundred and twenty-nine;
Now, re-cast, I weakly whine!

III. Fifteen hundred used to be
My date, but since they melted me
'Tis only eighteen fifty-three.

IV. Henry Hopkins got me made,
And I summon folk as bade;
Not to much purpose, I'm afraid!

V. I likewise; for I bang and bid
In commoner metal than I did,
Some of me being stolen and hid.

VI. I, too, since in a mould they flung me,
Drained my silver, and rehung me,
So that in tin-like tones I tongue me.

VII. In nineteen hundred, so 'tis said,
They cut my canon off my head,
And made me look scalped, scraped, and dead.

VIII. I'm the peal's tenor still, but rue it!
Once it took two to swing me through it:
Now I'm rehung, one dolt can do it.


## EPITAPH ON A PESSIMIST

I'm Smith of Stoke, aged sixty-odd,
I've lived without a dame
From youth-time on; and would to God
My dad had done the same.

(From the French and Greek)


## A PARTING-SCENE

The two pale women cried,
But the man seemed to suffer more,
Which he strove hard to hide.
They stayed in the waiting-room, behind the door,
Till startled by the entering engine-roar,
As if they could not bear to have unfurled
Their misery to the eyes of all the world.

A soldier and his young wife
Were the couple; his mother the third,
Who had seen the seams of life.
He was sailing for the East I later heard.
– They kissed long, but they did not speak a word;
Then, strained, he went. To the elder the wife in tears
'Too long; too long!' burst out. ('Twas for five years.)

# SHORTENING DAYS AT THE HOMESTEAD

The first fire since the summer is lit, and is smoking into the
    room:
  The sun-rays thread it through, like woof-lines in a loom.
  Sparrows spurt from the hedge, whom misgivings appal
That winter did not leave last year for ever, after all.
    Like shock-headed urchins, spiny-haired,
    Stand pollard willows, their twigs just bared.

Who is this coming with pondering pace,
Black and ruddy, with white embossed,
His eyes being black, and ruddy his face
And the marge of his hair like morning frost?
    It's the cider-maker,
    And appletree-shaker,
And behind him on wheels, in readiness,
His mill, and tubs, and vat, and press.

# SONG TO AN OLD BURDEN

The feet have left the wormholed flooring,
    That danced to the ancient air,
    The fiddler, all-ignoring,
Sleeps by the gray-grassed cello-player:
Shall I then foot around around around,
    As once I footed there!

The voice is heard in the room no longer
    That trilled, none sweetlier,
    To gentle stops or stronger,
Where now the dust-draped cobwebs stir:
Shall I then sing again again again,
    As once I sang with her!

The eyes that beamed out rapid brightness
    Have longtime found their close,
    The cheeks have wanned to whiteness
That used to sort with summer rose:
Shall I then joy anew anew anew,
    As once I joyed in those!

O what's to me this tedious Maying,
    What's to me this June?
    O why should viols be playing
To catch and reel and rigadoon?
Shall I sing, dance around around around,
    When phantoms call the tune!

# 8

*from*

## WINTER WORDS IN VARIOUS
## MOODS AND METRES

# PROUD SONGSTERS

The thrushes sing as the sun is going,
    And the finches whistle in ones and pairs,
And as it gets dark loud nightingales
      In bushes
Pipe, as they can when April wears,
    As if all Time were theirs.

These are brand-new birds of twelve-months' growing,
Which a year ago, or less than twain,
No finches were, nor nightingales,
      Nor thrushes,
But only particles of grain,
    And earth, and air, and rain.

## 'I AM THE ONE'

I am the one whom ringdoves see
    Through chinks in boughs
    When they do not rouse
    In sudden dread,
But stay on cooing, as if they said:
    'Oh; it's only he.'

I am the passer when up-eared hares,
    Stirred as they eat
    The new-sprung wheat,
    Their munch resume
As if they thought: 'He is one for whom
    Nobody cares.'

Wet-eyed mourners glance at me
    As in train they pass
    Along the grass
    To a hollowed spot,
And think: 'No matter; he quizzes not
    Our misery.'

I hear above: 'We stars must lend
    No fierce regard
    To his gaze, so hard
    Bent on us thus, –
Must scathe him not. He is one with us
    Beginning and end.'

# AN UNKINDLY MAY

A shepherd stands by a gate in a white smock-frock:
He holds the gate ajar, intently counting his flock.

The sour spring wind is blurting boisterous-wise,
And bears on it dirty clouds across the skies;
Plantation timbers creak like rusty cranes,
And pigeons and rooks, dishevelled by late rains,
Are like gaunt vultures, sodden and unkempt,
And song-birds do not end what they attempt:
The buds have tried to open, but quite failing
Have pinched themselves together in their quailing.
The sun frowns whitely in eye-trying flaps
Through passing cloud-holes, mimicking audible taps.
'Nature, you're not commendable today!'
I think. 'Better tomorrow!' she seems to say.

That shepherd still stands in that white smock-frock,
Unnoting all things save the counting his flock.

## CHRISTMASTIDE

The rain-shafts splintered on me
   As despondently I strode;
The twilight gloomed upon me
   And bleared the blank high-road.
Each bush gave forth, when blown on
   By gusts in shower and shower,
A sigh, as it were sown on
   In handfuls by a sower.

A cheerful voice called, nigh me,
   'A merry Christmas, friend!' –
There rose a figure by me,
   Walking with townward trend,
A sodden tramp's, who, breaking
   Into thin song, bore straight
Ahead, direction taking
   Toward the Casual's gate.

## EVENING SHADOWS

The shadows of my chimneys stretch afar
Across the plot, and on to the privet bower,
And even the shadows of their smokings show,
And nothing says just now that where they are
They will in future stretch at this same hour,
Though in my earthen cyst I shall not know.

And at this time the neighbouring Pagan mound,
Whose myths the Gospel news now supersede,
Upon the greensward also throws its shade,
And nothing says such shade will spread around
Even as today when men will no more heed
The Gospel news than when the mound was made.

# THROWING A TREE

## NEW FOREST

The two executioners stalk along over the knolls,
  Bearing two axes with heavy heads shining and wide,
  And a long limp two-handled saw toothed for cutting
    great boles,
And so they approach the proud tree that bears the death-
    mark on its side.

  Jackets doffed they swing axes and chop away just above
    ground,
  And the chips fly about and lie white on the moss and
    fallen leaves;
  Till a broad deep gash in the bark is hewn all the way
    round,
And one of them tries to hook upward a rope, which at last
    he achieves.

  The saw then begins, till the top of the tall giant shivers:
  The shivers are seen to grow greater each cut than before:
  They edge out the saw, tug the rope; but the tree only
    quivers,
And kneeling and sawing again, they step back to try pulling
    once more.

  Then, lastly, the living mast sways, further sways: with
    a shout
  Job and Ike rush aside. Reached the end of its long
    staying powers
  The tree crashes downward: it shakes all its neighbours
    throughout,
And two hundred years' steady growth has been ended in
    less than two hours.

## LYING AWAKE

You, Morningtide Star, now are steady-eyed, over the east,
    I know it as if I saw you;
You, Beeches, engrave on the sky your thin twigs, even the
        least;
    Had I paper and pencil I'd draw you.
You, Meadow, are white with your counterpane cover of
     dew,
    I see it as if I were there;
You, Churchyard, are lightening faint from the shade of the
     yew,
    The names creeping out everywhere.

## SILENCES

There is the silence of a copse or croft
     When the wind sinks dumb,
     And of a belfry-loft
When the tenor after tolling stops its hum.

And there's the silence of a lonely pond
     Where a man was drowned,
     Nor nigh nor yond
A newt, frog, toad, to make the merest sound.

But the rapt silence of an empty house
     Where oneself was born,
     Dwelt, held carouse
With friends, is of all silences most forlorn!

Past are remembered songs and music-strains
     Once audible there:
     Roof, rafters, panes
Look absent-thoughted, tranced, or locked in prayer.

It seems no power on earth can waken it
    Or rouse its rooms,
    Or its past permit
The present to stir a torpor like a tomb's.

## 'A GENTLEMAN'S SECOND-HAND SUIT'

Here it is hanging in the sun
    By the pawn-shop door,
A dress-suit – all its revels done
    Of heretofore.
Long drilled to the waltzer's swing and sway,
    As its tokens show:
What it has seen, what it could say
    If it did but know!

The sleeve bears still a print of powder
    Rubbed from her arms
When she warmed up as the notes swelled louder
    And livened her charms –
Or rather theirs, for beauties many
    Leant there, no doubt,
Leaving these tell-tale traces when he
    Spun them about.

Its cut seems rather in bygone style
    On looking close,
So it mayn't have bent it for some while
    To the dancing pose:
Anyhow, often within its clasp
    Fair partners hung,
Assenting to the wearer's grasp
    With soft sweet tongue.

Where is, alas, the gentleman
    Who wore this suit?
And where are his ladies? Tell none can:
    Gossip is mute.

Some of them may forget him quite
    Who smudged his sleeve,
Some think of a wild and whirling night
    With him, and grieve.


# HE NEVER EXPECTED MUCH

## [or]

### A CONSIDERATION

### [*A reflection*] ON MY EIGHTY-SIXTH BIRTHDAY

Well, World, you have kept faith with me,
    Kept faith with me;
Upon the whole you have proved to be
    Much as you said you were.
Since as a child I used to lie
Upon the leaze and watch the sky,
Never, I own, expected I
    That life would all be fair.

'Twas then you said, and since have said,
    Times since have said,
In that mysterious voice you shed
    From clouds and hills around:
'Many have loved me desperately,
Many with smooth serenity,
While some have shown contempt of me
    Till they dropped underground.

'I do not promise overmuch,
    Child; overmuch;
Just neutral-tinted haps and such,'
    You said to minds like mine.
Wise warning for your credit's sake!
Which I for one failed not to take,
And hence could stem such strain and ache
    As each year might assign.

## THE SECOND VISIT

Clack, clack, clack, went the mill-wheel as I came,
And she was on the bridge with the thin hand-rail,
And the miller at the door, and the ducks at mill-tail;
I come again years after, and all there seems the same.

And so indeed it is: the apple-tree'd old house,
And the deep mill-pond, and the wet wheel clacking,
And a woman on the bridge, and white ducks quacking,
And the miller at the door, powdered pale from boots to
      brows.

But it's not the same miller whom long ago I knew,
Nor are they the same apples, nor the same drops that dash
Over the wet wheel, nor the ducks below that splash,
Nor the woman who to fond plaints replied, 'You know I do!'


## 'WE ARE GETTING TO THE END'

We are getting to the end of visioning
The impossible within this universe,
Such as that better whiles may follow worse,
And that our race may mend by reasoning.

We know that even as larks in cages sing
Unthoughtful of deliverance from the curse
That holds them lifelong in a latticed hearse,
We ply spasmodically our pleasuring.

And that when nations set them to lay waste
Their neighbours' heritage by foot and horse,
And hack their pleasant plains in festering seams,
They may again – not warely, or from taste,
But tickled mad by some demonic force. –
Yes. We are getting to the end of dreams!

## HE RESOLVES TO SAY NO MORE

O my soul, keep the rest unknown!
It is too like a sound of moan
      When the charnel-eyed
      Pale Horse has nighed:
Yea, none shall gather what I hide!

Why load men's minds with more to bear
That bear already ails to spare?
      From now alway
      Till my last day
What I discern I will not say.

Let Time roll backward if it will;
(Magians who drive the midnight quill
      With brain aglow
      Can see it so)
What I have learnt no man shall know.

And if my vision range beyond
The blinkered sight of souls in bond,
      – By truth made free –
      I'll let all be.
And show to no man what I see.

# INDEXES

# INDEX OF TITLES

# INDEX OF TITLES

# INDEX OF FIRST LINES

*More poetry published by Penguins
is described on the following
pages*

# THE PENGUIN POETS

# THE PENGUIN POETS

### SOME ANTHOLOGIES

*The Penguin Book of Australian Verse*

EDITED BY R. J. HOWARTH, KENNETH SLESSOR
AND JOHN THOMPSON – D 40

*The Penguin Book of Canadian Verse*

EDITED BY RALPH GUSTAFSON – D 46

*The Penguin Book of English Verse*

EDITED BY JOHN HAYWARD – D 32

*The Penguin Book of French Verse (4 volumes)*

EDITED BY B. WOLEDGE, GEOFFREY BRERETON AND
ANTHONY HARTLEY – D 50, D 43, D 33, D 47

*The Penguin Book of German Verse*

EDITED BY L. W. FORSTER – D 36

*The Penguin Book of Italian Verse*

EDITED BY GEORGE KAY – D 37

*The Penguin Book of Modern American Verse*

EDITED BY GEOFFREY MOORE – D 22*

*The Penguin Book of New Zealand Verse*

EDITED BY ALLEN CURNOW – D 45

*The Penguin Book of Spanish Verse*

EDITED BY J. M. COHEN – D 30

The Foreign anthologies have English prose translations
of each poem at the foot of the page

* Not for sale in the U.S.A.